I0022727

HELL ON WHEELS

HELL ON WHEELS

Disabled Dominants

Edited by Raven Kaldera

Alfred Press
Hubbardston, Massachusetts

Alfred Press
12 Simond Hill Road
Hubbardston, MA 01452

Hell on Wheels: Disabled Dominants
© 2012 by Raven Kaldera
ISBN 978-0-9828794-4-3

Cover Photography by John Riedell

All rights reserved. Unless otherwise specified,
no part of this book may be reproduced in any form
or by any means without the permission of the author.

Printed in cooperation with
Lulu Enterprises, Inc.
860 Aviation Parkway, Suite 300
Morrisville, NC 27560

*Dedicated to my weasel-boy,
whose devoted service gives me
effectiveness in the world.
We are the best team ever.*

Contents

Foreword

This book came about partly because a progressive genetic illness pushed me into a place of disability, partly because I saw other disabled dominants struggling with the physical spaces and community myths of the BDSM demographic, and partly because I am determined to be an activist for everything that I am, in some way. That means building bridges between communities — long, slender threads that become stronger and sturdier as more and more people pass across them. It means speaking up in a way that will be the most effective for the future goals that you want to put in place, which is the purpose of this book. It exists to tell the stories of actual disabled dominants, to provide inspiration for others like them, important coping tips for both them and their s-types, and a window into this world for people who are, as some of my friends put it, "temporarily able-bodied".

If this book is a bridge across communities, it is only a limited one. *Hell On Wheels* deals only with physical disabilities, and only with dominants. I considered expanding its scope, but decided against it ... because I feel that submissives with physical disabilities, and both dominants and submissives with mental illnesses and neurological problems really need their own books, where the proper space and focus can be given to their own specific issues. I hope to see those books come out in the future; with luck, this will be a seed to begin a grove of trees.

The first thing that people need to understand is that not all dominants need to be tall and strong and able to throw someone to the ground. It's true that when you have a disability, you're at a disadvantage for any kind of dating, but it's especially true when it comes to being a BDSM dominant looking for a submissive. While disabled s-types (submissives and slaves) have their own problems with getting significant others, it's less socially penalizing to be an s-type with a disability, because it's seen as a weakness, and it's more acceptable for s-types to have weaknesses. Or perhaps I should say that in the mythos of the BDSM demographic, it is often ridiculously, unrealistically unacceptable for dominants to have any weaknesses whatsoever.

There's a kernel of need and fear at the bottom of that myth. When a person turns part or all of the authority over their life to someone else, they're in a very vulnerable place. It's understandable that in order to feel safe, they are going to want to believe that the person they've turned it over to is the strongest and most competent individual of all. A master or mistress who is often laid low by illness or cannot do many basic things for themselves may not make the s-type feel safe, utterly protected, and cared for on an irrational, emotional level … and, fair or not, that's often the level that needs to be satisfied before the s-type can fully trust enough to give themselves over.

There's also the fact that there is often (though not always) a strong sexual fetish component to power dynamic relationships. Physical strength and health are associated with dominance in the minds of many people, and they don't find the opposite sexy at all. While this too may seem unfair, it's important to take a deep breath and remember that sexual attraction is never fair. It's always fickle and subjective, and it wants what it wants regardless of what anyone might prefer intellectually.

In addition, submissives and slaves each have their own internal scale as to what qualities mean "this person is superior" to them. Those qualities are not only extremely subjective and variable, they are often ruled by the aforementioned irrational level. For many, physical prowess is absolutely a requirement. They need a master who can literally wrestle them down, or they don't feel moved to submit. On one particular online list for people in power dynamics, someone asked whether the s-types on the list would consider someone with dwarfism as a master. Fully half of them said no; for them, only a master who was larger, stronger, and able to dominate them physically could inspire them to surrender and obedience.

On the other hand, that left half of the s-types on the list saying, "Yes, I might, if it was the right person with the right dominant attitude." Not everyone has a "superior" list that includes physical aspects. For some, the M-type needs to be smarter than them, and able to out-think them. For some, the dominant needs to be fascinating and inspiring, or more experienced and knowledgeable about the world, or better able to hold to their moral code and be a good person. For others — like my own slaveboy — what's "superior" is a dominant with far better self-control and greater willpower than the s-types in question. All of these qualities are quite achievable by dominants with physical disabilities, and they are often the reasons that our s-types give for why they follow us.

The dominants who write these essays are brave, indomitable people who do not let their physical difficulties get in the way of taking charge of their lives ... and the lives of others. Their sheer willpower, and their adaptability to the unfairnesses of life, shines through. The submissives and slaves who write about their beloved and respected masters and mistresses are loyal and dedicated people who do not let their M-type's limitations get in the way of their own dedication. This is a book of pure courage and devotion, an inspiration to anyone who worries that brutal life circumstances will prevent them from getting what they want.

One note on terminology: Several of the authors in this anthology, myself included, will often use the word "spoons" to indicate a discrete unit of body energy. This analogy was first made by Christine Miserandino, the creator of the website http://www.butyoudontlooksick.com, an online support network for people with chronic illnesses. She describes the "spoon theory" in an article on the website, where she tells the story of being in a late-night diner and trying to explain to a friend what it was like to live with a chronic illness. She grabbed up the spoons from nearby tables and used them as an abstract example — each spoon represented a unit of energy needed to do some small and basic thing such as wash, dress, or eat — and some days there weren't enough "spoons" to do much of anything. Since then, many people with chronic illnesses and disabilities that impact their energy levels (and thus their ability to manage everyday activities) have referred to their "units of energy" as "spoons", as in "I've only got two spoons left, so I'd better get home while I can still drive."

People now wish each other more spoons, and even give away little spoon-shaped pins as gifts. You'll see that term used throughout the book by various authors who struggle daily to make the most of their limited spoons.

May you all be as healthy as it's possible to be, with more spoons than you ever expected, and have joy in bed and out of it, in the dungeon and out of it, in the community and out of it, in the circle of family and out of it, and in each others' hearts and minds.

RAVEN KALDERA
MAY 15, 2012

Being A Disabled Dominant

Disability and Mastery
Del Schlosser

My name is Del, and I'm a monster.

I've been part of the BDSM scene since the late 90s. I started out as a sub, did some pro work for some time, and as time progressed it became clear to me that I was not in fact a submissive but a top. The longer I topped, the more I got people coming to me who felt compelled to offer me acts of service, so I sought out various mentors who taught me what it was to be a dominant and a master.

Physically, things have not been easy for me. I have an anomalous and undiagnosed neurological disorder that causes muscular and pain difficulties, as well as occasional cognitive difficulties. I have moderate mobility issues and varying amounts of stamina. I suffer from moderate to severe chronic pain on a regular basis, and I am sometimes struck with aphasia. (That's not being able to find the right word at the right time. I may even know what word I want to say, but somehow I can't communicate it, which is not handy when I might want to communicate to a bottom that something has gone wrong.) I've spent more time in hospitals than I want to think about. Sometimes I am confined mostly to bed for days, and can't make it up stairs. It's a huge effort to get to an event, and if the play is late at night, I'm often too exhausted and in too much pain by that time to go. Constant pain management and medication are facts of my life.

When I think of the perfect dominant, I think of a tall, strong imposing figure with an aura of mastery and control about them. They are always completely physically able, and perhaps even partly superhuman. Of course, I don't resemble that in any way. It took me a long time to realize that just because this was my mental image of a dominant didn't mean that I couldn't be a dominant anyhow. I came to this understanding through accepting acts of service from those who offered. I could feel the power dynamic between myself and the sub, and I came to understand that the power exchange was all about the two people involved, and what was going on in their heads rather than their bodies.

One thing I have learned is that the power exchange between two people develops as a unique organism, and it doesn't have to resemble anyone else's relationship. Something that can look like weakness can actually be turned into a strength if you can find a new way to define it. For example, it took me a long time to accept physical service, such as helping me to dress, tying my shoes, or interacting with my body in a way that reminds me of weakness. However, reframing those actions as intimate acts of service harks back to Victorian times when servants would get their ladies into their corsets. They become a way that the submissive gets to do things with the dominant that most people doesn't. The person receiving the service is very definitely the dominant, and it can be an intimate and bonding act between the two people.

The next thing that I learned was how to create the "dominant aura". There is an energetic field that I can put on, regardless of how I feel, that radiates to my submissive, "This is your dominant speaking, and now you are in submissive mode, and we are heady in our power dynamic." I've learned to do that even when lying in a hospital bed. I can put that energy forward, and it will drop her and remind her that she is still in service to me. I can also do that during play, so that if for whatever reason I don't have the energy to do SM as intensely as I would like, I can put on that dominant aura, and no matter how light we play, she takes it as a masochistic activity because the aura helps to enhance the intensity of the experience.

Power is not necessarily a physical thing. We think of power as related to strength, including physical, mental, and emotional. However, power comes in many flavors, and if you get hung up on one of them, you may miss the opportunity to have power over another human being. If you're all hung up on being the biggest, baddest top of all whose power is in having strenuous scenes, but your body won't cooperate with that, you may miss out on the rituals and protocols that can create a meaningful power exchange and have nothing to do with your physical prowess.

Good power dynamics are organic beings. Even through your disability, you will have to find your own unique ways to feed both your own mindset as a dominant and your submissive's mindset, ways that are within your ability to manage. For some those may be rituals, for some those may be acts of service, for some those may be protocol, for some those may be language or just acts of deference. It doesn't cost me any "spoons" to tell my submissive that she can't sit on furniture or to have rules about how to address me.

When you feel like you have a weakness that they must cope with — something you need because of your disability, or something you can't do — you have to learn to reframe and to refocus that, remembering that you are the one who is in control. You may not be in control of your disability, but you are in control of the way in which it is received and treated. In the beginning of my relationship with my submissive, I noticed that she treated my body with kid gloves, and was very protective of how others interacted with my body, especially when my pain was bad. That made me feel weak, because it made me feel like she held the control over how she and others would interact with my body. So I told her that my body belongs to me and not her, and that I would instruct her if it required any different handling than anyone else's body, and only then was she to treat it differently. Since then, one of the services I've had her do is to watch for when people are trying to coddle me. She will take them aside and tell them, "If you want to be Del's friend or to actually be helpful, treat Del as though health isn't an issue, and Del will let you know if he needs any special treatment."

Another difficulty we went through was that she would turn down offers for play because she feared that I would be feeling too poorly or didn't have enough stamina at the moment. I reminded her that she should take up the offer whenever possible, because I could stop making those offers at any time if I chose. To decide when I was well enough for play was under my control and my power.

If you're going to be a sub for a disabled dominant, you need to learn that there is a marked difference between a PCA (personal care assistant) and a submissive. I think that some people are attracted to offering service to disabled dominants because they really want to become PCAs. In darker expressions, they may want to become subs to disabled doms because they have an underlying parental urge, and they want to lose themselves in the needs of the dominant. Then their own needs don't matter, and they can subsume themselves in the dominant's needs. That's why my sub has a job, and has her own life beyond taking care of me. The problem with that subsuming is that in some cases, it can desexualize things. I think it's important to remember that even when your dominant may not be in the best of moods or physical condition, it may still be useful to keep bringing sexual or SM energy into your interactions. Power-dynamic-related activities can help keep those relationships well-defined. I've had D/s relationships where it became all about the physical care and there was no sexual spark, and no deep power dynamic — they just wanted to take care of someone. That's the difference between seeing the dominance in a disabled person and wanting to submit to that, and seeing the disability in a dominant and wanting to take care of that.

Also, be flexible about what the dominant wants to do themselves on any given day. When a dominant asserts more control over what makes them functional, be it mobility equipment, medicine, or physical therapy, the submissive should not take it as a lack of trust in them. Sometimes exerting that control is all you have to feel human — for example, I may not want you to push my wheelchair today because moving myself through time and space makes me feel more human. Sometimes the best thing that a submissive can do for a disabled dominant is not to make things easier or less impactful, but to find ways to make their dominant feel more whole and more human. It's tempting to default to "How do I make this easier for them?" instead of checking with them to see what they really want in the situation. I may be feeling better today and want to challenge myself, and I need to be able to communicate that instead of having her just do what she thinks is best for me.

There many services that the submissive of a disabled dominant can offer, but they have to be offered in a way that bonds rather than undermines the power exchange. First, there's administering medication. This can be done with the impersonal (and depersonalizing) attitude of a nurse, or it can be done with a positive service attitude. Over time, there have been various submissives with whom I have practiced varying levels of control with my medication. For some, they were in complete control of it; for some, they held it but I decided when to take it; for some I did everything myself with timers and such. I've had a couple of bad incidents with subs and medication. Once I was traveling with a past sub who was in charge of packing up my belongings, and she left all of my medications behind at the hotel. I went back and forth wondering about whether or not that was a level of control I was willing to relinquish to her, or if it was a simple mistake that I needed to correct, forgive, and move on.

Right now my service sub does not administer my meds unless I absolutely need her to. Because she doesn't live with me, it's hard for her to remember when I take which medication, and it's easier for me to do it; however, there have been times when I've needed her help with it. As an example, I am pretty averse to anal play, but once I was stuck at an event where I needed a suppository inserted. I usually let my husband do that, because I have a more intimate relationship with him. However, he wasn't there and my sub was, so I had to find a way to make this feel like service while doing something that made me extremely uncomfortable. I told her that I was going to share something with her as a reward for how much I trusted her with administering my medications, and that she would be allowed to administer the suppository because she had been proven trustworthy. That made it a very positive bonding experience for both of us.

Second, I use my sub to judge the accessibility of a place or event where we plan to go. I will send her ahead of me to check out the chairs in the room, how much walking is involved, whether they expect us to stand, whether there is parking close to the building, etc. Then she comes back to me and reports, and we work out a plan of how to make it more accessible for me.

I travel a lot for events, and I almost always travel with her. She does all the packing, all the driving, all the unpacking, all the arranging, and all the repacking. It works out fine; our only problem has been with her not being entirely certain at first how she should arrange things. Her idea of where things belong and my idea of where things belong has not gotten to a perfect place yet — but we're working on it.

Third, one of the best services she provides for me, and one that I really appreciate, is simply her presence. When she has a free weekend, she comes and sits by my bedside and entertains herself, in case something arises where I might need help. Even if she is off doing other things during the weekend, I can call her and say that I predict I will need help because of whatever circumstance is going to arise, and she will cancel her plans and come sit at my bedside in case I need help.

Submissives who serve disabled dominants should have at least one support person that they can turn to, particularly if the dominant's needs become serious enough that burn-out threatens. Getting support elsewhere can help them to come to their service with a clean head and heart, which is not something that humans are used to doing. They need their own social support system to endure it. It might mean going to events when their dominant can't, in order to keep connections in the local BDSM community. If they can be open and honest about their relationship and its challenges, they can feel like they are being held by their community when times are hard.

It's not easy being disabled in much of the BDSM demographic. I know that for some communities, I find discreet ways to suggest applicable suggestions to make their playspaces more friendly and accessible. I don't expect every public space to be completely wheelchair-accessible and all their equipment to be adapted for people with limited mobility, but I do look for small ways to make things accessible myself. That includes making my own equipment — be it a wheelchair or a cane or a toybag — better able to move in those spaces. As an example, my piercing gear is in a box that breaks down into smaller tables, so if I need to vary the way that my workspace is laid out in order to engage in a prolonged piercing scene, I have the ability to create my own space rather than relying on whatever the dungeon might have to offer.

I feel that part of the way I assert control — both over my sub and over my own disability — is that before I attend an event, I contact the organizer and talk about ways the event can be made more accessible. For instance, some events will allow me to bring my sub for free, because without her it would be a hardship for me to attend. It is not shameful to be your own advocate and to make sure that when you attend these events you will be seen and accepted by the other attendees, because your disability needs have already been met and are not the focus of your attendance at the event.

There's also the question of people who fetishize the disabled. This is a decision that every disabled dominant will have to make for themselves, and it will come down to whether they are all right with being objectified. I personally feel that I would rather be seen as a whole human being, and not just as my mobility equipment and neurological disorders, and if someone is only looking at that I'm less willing to engage with them. For some people, however, it may be healing to have someone find them attractive because of, not in spite of, the fact that they are in a wheelchair.

To be someone who is willing to take up the banner of changing public perception — because not everyone is — you need to do what you do in public, loudly and deliberately attracting attention. When you get that attention, calmly answer questions if they are appropriate. If they are inappropriate, courteously explain why they are inappropriate, and do not answer them. For example, if someone assumes that my submissive is in control because she is filling out my paperwork for me (because of the assumption that filling out paperwork should be a dominant activity), and I am made aware of that assumption, I will gently but firmly explain to them that this is an act of service and that perhaps their mindset could use some readjusting.

For some dominants, it may be emotionally necessary for them to refrain from going out in public when they are at their worst, so that they will be able to maintain their image as a dominant and convey that to the public. They may need to pick and choose their events carefully in order to keep that going. I know that in my local scene there is a lot of peer pressure to go to every play party and kinky barbecue and meeting, and to be involved with many different groups. I've found that it is better for me to be discerning about which events are the most accessible to my physical needs, and best serve the needs of my power dynamic. This means that I will turn down events that don't make space for my needs, or fall at times of especially poor health. After all, these are supposed to be enjoyable activities that help us bond in our power dynamic, and if they do neither, there's no point in going. Never feel guilty about saving your spoons for the event where you know you'll have fun.

Mastery And Chronic Illness
Raven Kaldera

A few years ago I was diagnosed with systemic lupus erythematosus, generally known as lupus — the Wolf that devours us — to those of us with the disease. Lupus is the granddaddy of autoimmune diseases, where a person's own immune system attacks various parts of their body by turns — skin, bones, tissue, organs, anything it can reach. It is chronic, progressive, incurable, and eventually fatal, although it can be held back in some cases for many years. I'd had the first symptoms in my early teens, but lupus is notoriously difficult to diagnose because it can look like so many other random disorders in turn.

I was chronically ill throughout my teens and twenties, dealing not only with my mysterious illness but with a few other diagnosed genetic problems — an intersex condition caused by secondary congenital adrenal hyperplasia, skeletal malformations, a seizure disorder, a hiatal hernia, a mild case of Tourette syndrome, gender dysphoria, colitis, and slowly growing multiple chemical sensitivies. These last two problems would eventually turn out to be caused by the lupus, but the others were unrelated. I joked about how I was a deformed mutant — *Superior Mutants Unite!* — but it was the kind of joke that you laugh about in order to keep from crying.

Eventually the intersex condition — and the gender dysphoria — led me to get sex reassignment from female to male, and to my surprise the testosterone I began to inject actually made my mysterious illness better for about ten years. (I would later discover that this was because lupus is exacerbated by estrogen, among other things.) During this period of relative health I was a fairly active person, running around on my farm and heaving haybales. I took on a lot of work projects and was convinced that life would only get better physically.

Also during this time, I met the man who would eventually become my slave. Joshua started out as a farm intern, got "upgraded" to a lover, and then told me that there would be no greater honor than to be my boy. Within a year he had relocated to live with me and was my full-time slave.

He was the first s-type I'd ever had who was both deeply submissive and deeply service-oriented, and the first person who was serious about dedicating themselves to making my life easier and more comfortable.

We had a couple of good years, and then illness struck on both sides. His was brutal but treatable; that story will be told in a future book in this series, but suffice it to say that we got him treatment and it became only a periodic annoyance. However, my own health decided to plummet at the same time. The lupus attacked my skin, joints, guts, lungs, and liver, and the organ involvement was serious enough that my doctor of the time was finally able to diagnose it properly. The illness had progressed past the ability of the testosterone injections to counter, and the chemical sensitivities had rendered me allergic to most of the drugs used for its treatment. I was allergic to corticosteroids, and to the entire family of non-steroidal anti-inflammatories — aspirin, ibuprofen, etc. The Tourette syndrome also made me resistant to opiate-derived drugs — not an uncommon anecdotal side effect — so I was suddenly thrust into a life of chronic pain and exhaustion with no remedies in sight.

Medication-resistant lupus does not have a very good prognosis. In fact, the rheumatologist basically shrugged and sent me home, telling me to check into the hospital if it got bad enough. For about a year, I stewed in the unfairness of it all. I vacillated between doing nothing because I was hoping that this would be a temporary situation that would resolve itself, and doing nothing because I was too disheartened to face the inevitability. I refused to think of myself as disabled, even when the rheumatoid arthritis caused by the lupus made it increasingly difficult to get around. I was just having some difficulties for the moment, I told myself. Stupid as it was, it was an important part of my process. I needed to swim in that space and mourn what I was losing, at least for a little while, before I could move on. I had to adjust my identity from that of a person who struggled with a few physical problems to that of someone who has become disabled. I also had to come to terms with the fact that the lupus would probably kill me, if I wasn't hit by a bus, and that every year I could fight it off was a blessing. I had to get right with pain and death, because they would be hovering in the background for the rest of my life, and sometimes outright sharing my bed.

This was a terribly difficult period for my slaveboy, because he saw me suffering and not being my usual decisive self. When a master is stricken down by illness, it can be terrifying for the slave who has centered their entire life around them. Even if the illness isn't fatal, the fact that it can take the master out of commission for a period of time is frightening enough. No matter how dominant I may feel myself to be, when I'm having a bad lupus flare, I know that my judgment is off. Sometimes I can't do anything but lie in bed; the pain and fatigue cloud my mind and it's all I can do to get to the bathroom and back. It may only last for the day, but that's a day when Joshua is effectively on his own and can get little or no direction from me. My obvious denial of the fact that this was going to be our daily fight for the rest of my life also bewildered him. At one point he raged about it to Eli, a friend of ours who is a disability activist with cerebral palsy; Eli peaceably told him that this was a part of the process that I had to come to terms with, and that I'd do it in my own time.

At some point I slowly broke through the wall and accepted my fate, and finally got my wheels under me — literally; it was the day that an arthritis attack got so bad that I couldn't get out of bed, and a friend brought an old wheelchair over for me to use. Getting that chair up the stairs to choir practice, it finally came home to me that this wasn't going to go away, and would probably only get worse, and I'd better get off my ass and start planning. After all, wasn't that the master's job? If I couldn't master this illness, I could master everything around it, and create a virtual exoskeleton so that I could continue to be effective in the world. To do this, however, I had to accept being disabled and everything that went with that understanding.

My slaveboy was the obvious core to use for this exoskeleton, but first I had to help him in his fear and worry. We began by creating specific protocols for him to resort to when I was temporarily in too bad a way to manage. *If this happens, do that; if that happens, do this. Interact with me in this way if I'm like that, in that way if I'm like this. If you think I may need help and I'm not asking for it because it hasn't occurred to me, ask me. If I say no, trust me — I may need to struggle through some things myself for my own sense of self-worth. If an emergency occurs, call this person or that person. If you need to feel my dominance and I'm too sick, do this ritual activity, and be mindful while you're doing it that it is my will that demands it, even when I'm out of commission for the moment.*

It's important to an s-type to know what is expected of them in any circumstance; the uncertainty, more than anything else, drove him crazy. I strongly recommend creating a series of protocols to hold them steady when you need to step down from the helm at the moment. If you create them well enough — assuming that you don't have an extremely high-need, high-maintenance s-type who can't function without constant micromanagement — you will be able to fall out of the saddle, have your period of starfishing on the ground, and then have them help you back onto the horse with the power dynamic still intact. My end of the agreement, however, was that I had to work my hardest at realistically assessing my situation and what I could rationally expect of myself at any given time, and communicate that to him clearly so that we'd be on the same page about the protocols to which he should revert.

The next year went by in a haze of planning. I arranged alternative health care for myself — acupuncture, herbs, eliminating allergens and chemicals from my life in order to quiet down my schizophrenic immune system. My boy drove me to appointments, made me special food, and packed my med-minder. I fought my way back from the edge of acute (organ-involved) lupus, and although I still live with the chronic low-grade symptoms, no one ever died from joint pain and fatigue. We planned an extension on the house with a ramp and wheel-in shower for the inevitable future, and we began to save money. (That plan will probably come to fruition as this book goes through the publishing process.) My boy adapted to being my personal care attendant, giving me injections and holding me up in the shower on difficult days, and I realized how wonderful it is for a disabled person to have a slave. Sooner or later I'd have had to hire help or be completely screwed, including for personal duties that would be humiliating for a stranger to deal with. My slave, on the other hand, was happy to do those intimate things; for him, they were just another service he could render me.

Joshua himself was at a point in his life where he was looking for a new career. He'd left his original career to be with me, and had been taking low-grade part-time jobs ever since. He wanted to go back to school for more marketable skills, especially since it was clear that I would never be holding down any kind of a regular job in my life, and writing doesn't pay that well. We talked about it, and we decided that massage therapy would be a good career for him — and also a boon to me; having my own in-house massage therapist meant that I would have at least some pain relief on demand and would never have to train a stranger in how to touch my difficult body. One "useful certification" led to another, and over the next three and a half years he was certified in massage therapy, acupressure shiatsu, moxibustion and cupping, and hospice care — and got a degree in complementary health care. He also learned tai ch'i in order to be able to walk me through it on my better days. It was all part of training him to be the perfect PCA — because what's the point of having a slave if you can't train them to be the best possible companion, in whatever way you need them to be?

Those three and a half years were hell on me, though. I made the plans, found the schools, arranged payment, and set him up with a packed schedule in order to get through all the training as quickly as possible. This meant that much of the time, he wasn't there to do his job for me when I needed him. I'd robbed myself of my apprentice PCA in order to build an expert version, and there were days when I sat alone and in pain in my house and literally cried over it. I reminded myself, however, that I'd chosen this path; it was short-term loss for long-term gain, and I was an adult and could suck it up. It was hard on him to see the toll that it took on me, and he would have quit if I'd let him — but I didn't. Being the master means being the one to see the long-term plan and stick to it, forcing both yourself and your s-types through the hard parts. Since I consider us to be a Team, I emphasized to him that the best way he could support me in this was to align himself with my plan, thus showing that he respected my decisions even when they were hard ones, and to be a responsible adult along with me. If we both had to suck it up, we would suck it up together.

I remember more than one night when I woke up at 2 a.m. in pain, knowing that if I awoke the sleeping slaveboy next to me, he might be able to help me out so that I could get back to sleep. The mental monologue went something like this: *He won't be awake for another four and a half hours. But I'm in pain now! I don't want to wait four and a half hours, lying here like this! I want my massage. But he's got an exam today, he has to be on his game, and if I wake him up now, he won't get enough sleep. I know what he's like on not enough sleep. And that would be sabotaging my own plan. But he's going to be upset at me when he wakes up and finds out that I lay here in pain for four and a half hours letting him sleep. He's going to feel like the worst boy ever, I know that because it's happened before. But I'm the master, it's my plan, and if I have to suffer for it — if we both have to suffer for it — so be it. To abandon my plan for no other reason than to make either of us feel temporarily better would be to undermine my own sense of mastery. I am convinced that it will be worth the suffering.*

And so it was. We got through the difficult times, and now I have a beautifully trained slaveboy who has learned how to perform the most humiliating and excruciating physical services for me with an attitude that makes them feel like a luxury service. (The massage therapy program had a lot of "spa-training".) He has literally become my body-servant, in the old Roman sense of the word — the slave whose job it is to take care of my extensive bodily needs, whatever they might be. He is also my hands and feet when I need them, not to mention the one who pushes my wheelchair on the really bad days. (We've joked about how much more fun it would be if he could be chained to the wheelchair, but sadly we must behave ourselves in public.)

As we've developed him into my "exoskeleton", our protocols have changed to support my disabilities, not some fetishized idea of how slaves are supposed to serve their masters in various "traditional" M/s communities. For example, my slave doesn't walk behind me. I have spatial dyslexia (meaning that I have a very hard time judging distances) and I often walk with a cane; the combination can lead to tripping over curbs and sudden ditches. His job is to walk a fair way ahead of me and scout the terrain; if he sees an obstacle that might give me trouble, he stops and waits for me to catch up, and then goes on ahead once he's helped me navigate it. We've nicknamed this "service weasel position" (because he's not a service *dog*, he's a weasel). We've rehearsed the most effective distance to keep between us, and it's his job to make sure that he stays aware of where I am and doesn't get too far ahead.

Of course, the fact that he's walking in front of me means that I get a lovely view of his very nice butt, and I've often deliberately put him in tight pants on days when I know that there will be a lot of service weasel position, so he's aware that he is not only doing me a service but being a sex object for my entertainment as well. It's one of the small ways in which we try to keep the heat going in our relationship. Disability can tend to eat up everyone's energy, and practical considerations can sometimes seem far more important than emotional intensity; if we're not careful, we can forget the juicy parts of the power dynamic. It's important, when building protocols around the master's disability, to throw in actions that reify the power dynamic whenever possible. For instance, some days it's hard for me to bend over and reach my feet, so he needs to wash them and help me get my boots on. Making this a submissive act — he kneels on the floor and is instructed to do each of these things with reverence and occasional kisses on feet and boots — reminds both of us of our position in this relationship, and the sweetness of the power dynamic that made us want to do it in the first place.

We've learned to brainstorm about ways in which he can make things just a little bit easier for me. My hiatal hernia means that I need to drink before I can eat, I can't stand for long periods or juggle a tray and a cane, and my multiple allergies mean that buffet situations are a minefield. When we're faced with this — which is not unusual for conferences of all sorts — I grab a seat and wait, so I won't have to look at food I may not be able to eat anyway. He follows the rules I've set up and brings me a beverage first, before anything else. Then he inspects the food, buttonholes the staff to find out about ingredients if necessary (which, during potlucks, has sometimes meant digging boxes out of the trash to read ingredient lists), assembles me a plate of "safe" food that he knows from experience and training that I'll like, and delivers it to my table. Each of these pieces came one at a time as I realized that something irked me. Sometimes, when your life is a study in frustrations, every tiny frustration that can be swept out of the way by diligent service really means a lot and can make the difference between a bearable day and an unbearable one.

One of the points that I need to make right now is that being the servant of a disabled dominant intensifies the need for strict obedience. When he is literally in charge of parts of my health care — for example, when he's filling my med minder or finding me non-allergenic food — even a simple mistake can be disastrous, and there is absolutely no room for deliberate disobedience or even carelessness. From talking to M/s couples where the s-type isn't expected to be all that obedient, we discovered that the s-type in these cases was usually brought up around adults with jobs where a screwup meant firing at worst and a bunch of apologies at best. In many cases, they expressed doubt that it was possible for someone to be expected to get through the week without screwing up something, and that an apology ought to be good enough for both parties to be able to move on.

In contrast, we found that many of the s-types who were much more stalwart in their commitment to obedience had been raised with adults who were in fields such as health care and medicine, law enforcement, firefighting, or the military — fields where, if you screwed up, someone might be injured or even die. If you are a doctor or a nurse or a police officer, it is not unreasonable to expect you to do your absolute best every day to refrain from making errors. The difference between ten and a hundred milligrams of a drug could be the difference between life and death, and a mere apology isn't going to cut it.

Recently a friend who is also a disabled dominant called me on the phone. My friend lives with his egalitarian spouse, and has a female submissive who is his part-time PCA. He also lives with chronic pain and takes fairly serious painkillers, and he is in a special pain-management program that dispenses drugs and makes sure that they aren't being sold for their street value. The problem was that his girl had been careless when unpacking the coolers after a trip to a kinky camping event, and hadn't looked closely at what she was throwing out. She'd pitched his whole supply of painkiller skin patches, and by the next afternoon when he needed another one, the trash had already gone to the dump. He was in terrible pain and full withdrawal and would be that way until the next day when more medication could be obtained; his spouse was frantically dealing with the insurance company and the pain clinic, trying to convince the skeptical doctors that they needed another refill. The whole situation was a nightmare, and while his girl was sorry, he didn't think that she understood the gravity of the situation. "I don't like to resort to punishment, but I'm wondering if beating her will actually get the point across, pain for pain," he said.

I had a better idea. It was important that she see the results of what she'd done, in living color. *Have her come over, as soon as you're up to it. You and your spouse need to sit down with her, and describe in excruciating detail what you've both just been through. Spare her no awful, humiliating moment. She gets no safeword from this scene, either; she has to listen to every word, as many times as you want to tell her about it. Then you tell her that since she obviously can't be trusted with your medication, you're withdrawing that responsibility from her. She'll be able to earn it back once she proves over time that she can be more careful. This will reify that being given responsibility for any part of your health is a privilege, and it can be withdrawn if she proves herself unable to be completely reliable, and that this withdrawal of privileges is really the worst punishment of all. It will also drive home to her just what kind of pain she can cause by being careless, and encourage her to do a more meticulous job. Talk to her about what would have to happen for her to be more effective in this way, and encourage her to implement those methods.*

Being the servant of a disabled dominant really has to be a No Fucking Up job. Yes, sometimes everyone makes mistakes, but it's never OK, and the underlying issue that created the mistake needs to be dealt with as quickly as possible. It's painful and humiliating enough for me to accept how incredibly dependent I am on my slave; one of the few things that makes this bearable is knowing that he is absolutely rock-solid dependable when it comes to anything that can affect my health. If I couldn't trust him in this way — if his disobedience showed me that he cared more for his own emotional whims than my well-being, or that he lacked basic self-control to that great an extent — it would permanently damage our relationship.

Although as the s-type has to be responsible about their part of the job of caring for the M-type's health, the M-type needs to take the primary responsibility. It's important for both people to remember that what is really going on is *not* that the s-type is caring for their master — it's that their master is *using them* to care for himself or herself. I cannot emphasize this enough. The s-type is not a caretaker, they are a tool, and they need to act that way. A common sign of both parties forgetting that this is the case is when the s-type starts to act in a parental way toward the M-type. Not only can this seriously cut down on sexual heat, it can also slowly erode the power dynamic and the s-type's respect for the M-type. It's not unusual for the basis of this problem to be fear on the part of the s-type — they see the disability as taking control away from their master, and that puts them in a vulnerable place, and they try to grab control by "mothering" their master (and sometimes crossing over into nagging and deciding what's "best" for the master), regardless of gender. However, having yet more power taken away is never what's best for the master, and it's certainly not what's best for the relationship, and well-meaning s-types need to keep this in mind at all times.

On the other hand, for the s-type to be able to keep from grabbing for that power over the frustrations visited by the disability, they have to be reassured that their master is actually taking responsibility themselves — and that reassurance must be done with words, not actions. They need to see that their dominant is realistic about the extent of their disability, and is organizing their life and priorities in such a way that they are as functional as possible. A healthy s-type would rather be ordered to do inconvenient and grubby activities for their dominant than to see them ignore the situation and do without. This means, as I learned the hard way and related earlier in this chapter, that the dominant has to squarely face the reality of their body and its future.

My personal experience is not one of being disabled from birth or a young age — and I'm hoping that this experience will be addressed more thoroughly by other people in this book — but of moving slowly from nondisabled to fairly inconvenienced to outright disability over a period of time. Unlike people who have never known anything else, people who lose their ability as adults often have to go through a period of mourning, and we can have a lot of resentment about facing our situation. I generally advise people in this situation — and especially those who are coping with chronic illness that isn't going to go away, and may or may not go into remission — that it's better to choose to organize your life and your future as if you will always be disabled (and make allowances for future decline, if that's a possibility) while keeping the project of attempting to get better as a side hobby to which you are particularly dedicated. This may entail reorganizing your whole life and asking hard questions about which parts of your life can keep going with the current level of debility. It may mean making hard decisions about what to triage.

When a chronic illness first comes on, everyone involved is usually in crisis mode, and there's an underlying assumption that if we deal with this crisis, it's going to go away and then we'll be back to "normal" — meaning whatever life was like before. For some temporary disabilities — like recovering from an accident where there can be full healing — that's a useful way to run things. For the onset of a chronic condition, however, that's the opposite of useful. The dominant needs to reassess their life and start taking the steps to create the "new normal". It's healthy for both partners to mourn the loss of what was, but then both of them need to get on board with implementing the new normal as quickly as possible. One helpful option for the dismayed dominant is to talk to other people with similar situations, and ask them how they reorganized their lives to take their chronic condition into account.

I found out quickly that having a chronic illness meant that I needed to be more organized than I'd been before. Organizing things is generally the master's job anyway, but we're all human and some of us are less skilled at it than others. Chronic illness means that you have less time and energy to spare, because more of it will be taken up by periods of coping with illness and maintaining your body. Don't skimp on allocating that time, because you'll pay for it in the end by missing things you wanted to do. If you're not sure how much time you need, experiment. You can bring your slave into the process by telling them to note down how much work you did on Day X, under what circumstances, and how much rest you needed afterwards. Sometimes someone else can be more objective about how much time something took. Be sure to stress, however, that their job is to be an *actual* neutral and objective observer, and not put their interpretations into the process. (Again, you're using them as a tool.) You might communicate to them that if they don't seem to be able to do that, you'll be forced to enlist someone else.

There are many useful tricks to getting as much life as possible out of what reduced time and energy you've got. For example, be sure to build slack into your schedule to be used for recuperation or catching up. Actually schedule things, all sorts of things, because the laissez-faire "I'll do it later" often means that it will never get done because you're laid low. Schedule in redundancies — if you know that you have to be well enough to go to the RMV this week or your license will expire, schedule in two possible times. If you manage it on the first try, you can always use the second slot for something else. Use single trips for multiple purposes — kill as many birds as possible with the few spoons that you have. Find activities that you can do when you're laid low, or perhaps three-quarters low, and have those set up within easy reach for you. (It's all the better if they're activities that you enjoy doing, or that will give you a feeling of accomplishment if only in small ways.)

It can also be important to learn to strike a balance between respecting your own new limitations and being able to push just a little further for reasons of self-mastery. There's a difference between saying, "I'm going to wait just an hour longer before taking that pain pill, because I want to see if I can manage," and saying, "I don't feel like I need my insulin today." Pushing your boundaries can be a good way to get ongoing physical feedback, and it can also build your self-confidence to take that one little risk. However, don't be stupid; some things are too big to risk, and playing with them is simply self-destructive. No slave wants to see their master being self-destructive; that's terrifying to them. That doesn't mean that your slave's fears should keep you from pushing yourself, but it does mean that you need to have some things in place first — like a considered risk-assessment approach that you've discussed with your health care providers and/or other experienced sufferers, and a Plan B if things go wrong and you make yourself worse.

If all of this seems too overwhelming at first, start with small moves. Triage one thing that you can do without, then add in one piece of compensation structure. See how this works, then triage another thing and/or add in another piece of structure. Keep doing this steadily, but don't slack off. This approach helps both of you slowly get used to the "new normal", but it also shows your s-type that you are actually doing what is necessary to get the ship's new direction under control. It's good to let them in on what you're doing in this direction and to find them ways that they can help you if possible, because it relieves their feeling of crisis and their need to grab for control if it's clear that you're taking control yourself in a calm and measured way. However, what's not helpful is their expressing unsolicited opinions as to how you ought to be doing it differently. Even solicited opinions might be required to be stated in a very neutral format, to drive home that they are a tool and not Mom. Just as the dominant needs to be very invested in showing the s-type that control is in good hands, the s-type needs to be very invested in helping the dominant feel like they are taking control in their own unique but still effective way.

Sex is often an issue when one's disability gets in the way of "traditional" positions of activities. Sometimes I'm so exhausted that I can't get out of bed, but I still want to have some sex. Having him "do me" as a service is nice, but sometimes both of us want to experience more of my control over him. One of the fun sexual activities that we've discovered is turning him into my porn movie — it doesn't take much energy for me to direct him to do all sorts of things to himself for my entertainment, and it's a way that he can feel my predatory gaze and be entirely under my will, even when I'm flat out on the bed. He's also learned to be a "helpful victim" — getting himself into positions where it will be easier for me to do things to him.

I'm lucky that my disability does not make me less attractive to my slaveboy. I am aware that many s-types would not serve someone who was not a good physical specimen, and I consider myself fortunate to have found someone to whom that doesn't matter. He's fairly sexually easygoing, meaning that while he prefers men (and calls himself homoflexible), he isn't fixated on a single type, nor is he turned off by unusual bodies. It's what's in my head that attracts him — my will, my honor, my faith, and my brilliantly sick and twisted mind. He is also skilled at finding ways to eroticize any situation and to remind me that a blowjob often makes things a little better for me as well, even when I can't remember that in the moment. We are both confident that no matter how decrepit I get, we'll be able to find ways to have kinky sex.

Where the disability gets in the way of sex — aside from general pain and exhaustion cutting down my ability to have it at all — is when I'm trying to fuck my other partners, who are kinky but not my slaves. (I'm polyamorous and part of a large, loving poly family.) Unlike my relationship with Joshua, I haven't spent years working on their heads and teaching them how to find erotic whatever it is that I happen to be able to give. I love them, but it's often difficult for them when I can't do the activities that they love, either on that given day or any longer at all. Bondage is hard for me on days when my hands are hurting and my grip isn't functioning so well. I can generally find a way to hurt someone no matter what, but standing for a flogging scene when they really want to be dangling from the ceiling on their toes isn't doable. I can only hold fucking positions that require me to be on my damaged knees for a very short time, and only on good days. In some of these cases, depending on how comfortable the other partner is with it, I'll call my slaveboy in to put them in bondage, stand there and make sure that they don't wiggle out, untie the knots when we're done, help buckle on harnesses, occasionally support me physically in a particular position, and of course hand me things when I need them. Depending on the level of medications in my system, my own plumbing might work just fine or not so well, and he is sometimes used as a "fluffer", getting things going so that I don't have to frustrate my other partners. He finds a certain amount of nonreciprocation on my part (and the resulting sexual frustration) to be erotic, so it's not a chore for him.

When it comes to public dungeons, I don't hide my disability. I rarely go to them these days (mostly for financial reasons) and of course if they're up multiple flights of stairs with no elevator, it's not happening. When I go to a dungeon to play with someone else, I definitely bring the boy to scout ahead, grab a station that will work best for me physically, arrange seating for me, adjust equipment (like lowering a sling or massage table), and lay toys out for me. When I go with him, I'm much more casual because we don't do a lot of formal SM with each other. I've walked into a dungeon with nothing but my slave and my standard aluminum cane, and put him on the floor to lick my boots and then whacked him with that cane. One of my favorite activities in such space is to put him on the floor and kick him around, which is physically difficult for me these days because I'm not as steady on my feet. Generally he'll check around and find a clear area next to an unused solid bondage frame, and I'll have one hand on the frame and the other on my cane, and he knows to stay within kickable range of me and not roll too far away. (Not that he *wants* to get away — again, he's a helpful victim.)

I've also tried to find ways to make myself feel slightly sexier even with everything I go through. I often need ankle braces when walking around hotels at kink conferences, so a friend gave me a pair of motocross boots with lots of shiny buckles and a hard plate on the front, and I modified them to be my ankle supports — much hotter than anything orthopedic. I'm working on getting custom-made Mad Max-style leg braces of steel and leather rather than standard white elastic or neoprene. I think of all the metal hardware as cyberpunk-ish rather than emphasizing my crip status. And yes, I want to tell everyone out there that it is possible to publicly top someone from a wheelchair, especially if you have a well-trained service slave to handcuff them to the arms of your chair and then pull you backwards and forwards at your command, while you make them crawl after you, whip them as they crawl, run them over, bang them up against the wall with the chair, and taunt them with salient points like, "This hurts? Honey, you don't fucking know what pain is! Let me show you my world!" Topping from a wheelchair means that the bottom knows you're not going to have any sympathy for whiny shit.

Except for the absolute worst days (which I spend asleep or in pain), I'm still a dominant person regardless of what's going on with me. I may be frustrated by my physical limitations, but I don't stop being the sort of person who likes to control my slave or receive service from him. He is the main tool that I use to control my environment and make it more comfortable for myself, as well as facilitating my own effectiveness in the face of disability. He also doesn't stop being the sort of person who likes to serve and be controlled, and the structure of rules and conditioning that I have built around him is as much a cage for him as an exoskeleton for me; it reminds him every day of how owned he actually is.

I once engaged in dialogue with a slave for whom it was very important to her sense of slavery that she needed her master more than he needed her. While I understand that everyone has different qualities that they need for a power dynamic relationship to work — and I respected that this was what she needed to feel enslaved — I was less patient with her inability to believe that any master who was dependent on their slave was really a master. It's true that without my slave, it would be like I'd lost my arms and legs, in a way — I wouldn't be intrinsically worthless as a human being, but I certainly would be royally screwed. It is also true that it was very hard for me to come to terms with being this dependent on any human being, even if I owned them. I didn't ever want to react with fear of him abandoning me, or refrain from asking for something because I felt that he had the power to tell me no. That would completely undermine our dynamic, and I think this was what the slavegirl was thinking of.

Instead, what I've done is to transfer the essence of power away from who needs whom more on a daily practical basis to who has the ability to change whom, and in what direction. I have had access to my slaveboy's mind through his transparency, and I've spent eleven years shaping and changing and polishing him, both as my slave and as a human being. I've done this with his enthusiastic collusion, and the process has become one of the main reifications of our power dynamic. On the other hand, he cannot return the favor. He can't change me in any way, even when he might like to. In a sense, I have full hands-on access to his soul, while his access to my soul is Look But Don't Touch. For us, this defines our roles more than how helpless one of us would be without the other. Power lies not with who has the arms and legs, but who has the control panel. (Any comic book Evil Overlord could tell you that, right?)

I also see it as a balance between the master's need and the master's will. If need exceeds will — if the master is in such dire need in general that it overrides their will to control the relationship — then the power dynamic is going to fall apart. However, my needs have never exceeded my will, because my will is just that big. That's why my slaveboy's efforts are not him "helping" me, but me using him to achieve my goals. It's all subject to my will, which is strong enough that nothing overruns it for more than a few hours at a time. That's why I'm a master. And isn't that why they respect us, after all?

My Life Of Kink And Disability
MastrKink

My interest in kinky sex has been a lifelong passion (or addiction) for over 40 years, dating back to the first bondage magazine I encountered. It was in a 7/eleven store showing a well-endowed woman tightly tied up in raw hemp rope on the cover. Her large breasts were jutting out like torpedoes and the apparent smile on her face caused a similar one on my own. My nervousness and excitement was only increased by the cute girl working the cash register who, as I went to pay for it, looked at the cover and gave me a smile which seemed to say, "Cool, I'd like that." I was hooked from that point on.

So off I went on a grand sexual adventure learning and perfecting my skills for BDSM sexual play. But once I reached my early thirties, the muscular dystrophy that I knew was waiting for me began to show its ugly head. Rope work became more frustrating as the inability to tie tight knots or undo them became the norm rather than the exception.

As the years went by, the legs that used to support me for what seemed like hours of fucking my partner while she was tied and helpless in some bizarre position became weaker, and I felt the need to hurry and get it over with before I had to stop and cause sexual frustration for both of us. Rope was replaced with straps or belts that were more easily unbuckled. My arms couldn't be used to hold or move my partner around like before, but rather I had to have her move into a position that would be more permanent than usual. The years flew past, and over time I made many small adjustments that I probably wasn't even aware of.

But slowly I realized that I was making a shift in the type of play that I wanted; it became more for convenience and ease as opposed to intense and quite physical. I played more head games to prolong foreplay, relying on verbal abuse or some type of humiliation or degradation play to take the place of physical efforts on my part.

As my arms grew weaker, and I was unable to use a whip for prolonged periods of time, I preferred to use harsher single tails or quirts to leave marks more quickly rather than take my time and build up to a red blush more slowly. Canes or switches became my preferred method since they made a more satisfying smack than a belt or multi-blade whip, since I could no longer develop the velocity needed for the same result.

I became unable to use the tightest clamps when my grip failed to be able to open them enough to get them over my slave's big nipples or labia, so I shifted to needles to achieve the same goal of harsh punishment for her. It was so much easier to grab one and push a needle through rather than struggle to squeeze the clamp open and then use heavy weights to give her the long dull ache that she craved over a longer period of time.

But that became the problem; as time passed and my physical weakness increased, it became more apparent that my substitutions weren't quite the same. The quick sting of a needle through her nipples wasn't the same as a long drawn out period of weights and clamps on her genitalia. While switches and canes worked for me emotionally and physically, she preferred building up more slowly with whips or paddles, then moving to a more intense type of play.

Other adjustments had to be made particular once my BPH and the medications to deal with that pretty much eradicated any erections. By then, I was using any means of extreme sexual play for our pleasures. I was using my fists, large toys, humiliation, and even bringing in other women to help satisfy our lust for BDSM sex. It wasn't the same, of course; there is no substitute for a hard cock squirting semen in your hole, or the inability to move when tied down, or having your partner be physically able to do what was necessary for his satisfaction. It began to seem that too much time was spent trying to do new activities and then failing at them. If you prefer scratchy rope wrapped tight against your skin, smooth leather isn't adequate; having your dominant hold your legs up and spread painfully wide doesn't feel the same as you having to do it for him.

Even though my sub would never say so, I suspect that most submissives have an image of a dominant being physically strong and imposing in their look to give that sense of dominance that they need. So having a dom that has to use a cane to get around the room or a wheelchair takes away from that.

My slave says that it seems to be harder for her to find that submissive role than it used to be. This is partly because she's concerned for my well-being in moving around and not falling (it was six stitches the last time it happened); her concern for my safety seems to overrule her desire for sex. She feels that she needs to be more of a caregiver at times. Since her desire was always for hard physical dominance and not as a domestic slave, it's not the same for her.

Personally, while I recognize that my physical appearance and abilities have changed dramatically over the past ten years, I still feel as creative and sexually energetic as ever. I feel as strong on the inside as ever, and recent life events have proved to me that I'm as hard a man as I ever was, despite the weak individual that the world sees before them. However, it's still a struggle not to succumb to feeling weak. It's hard to feel strong when it seems like it's too much work to enjoy the sexual play that we used to. I sometimes seem to spend more time figuring out ways to do what I want than actually doing them, and having your sub do most of the physical work takes away from the atmosphere of domination that drew us into the lifestyle in the first place. Perhaps it's just old age creeping up as well, and the libido is dying some on its own, but I suspect that some of the desire is leaving because the physical satisfactions just aren't there anymore either.

I was never much for attending munches or play parties until I had retired and had less fear that my secret life would cause me problems in my pubic life. By then I had to take into consideration that most locations for private events weren't likely to be ADA compliant. Public events at hotels or convention locations would be fine, but going to a private location that might have steps or low slung furniture that would be hard to get out of were out of the question. So once again limitations were placed on me because of my disability.

When my slave had a knee replaced this year, the problems that she had getting around in public and having to deal with low chairs or booths in a restaurant or bathrooms made her more aware of what I had been dealing with for a few years. People that are healthy and have full mobility have a very hard time truly understanding what some of us have to go through in life in order to enjoy it to the fullest.

One of the inspirations that I have used over the years has been the physicist Stephen Hawking. Here was a man that had a major disability since he was 21, yet he continued on to become a huge influence in science, married, and led a full and rich life. How could I not do the same? While I may have physical disabilities that limit my pleasure in some ways, it has never meant that I should give it up completely. I've lived my life that way sexually and in other aspects as well and have no plans to do less in the future.

It's not easy, mind you. My slave has been having increasing problems with her rheumatoid arthritis causing severe joint pain at times. So now we have to deal with that as well as my own disability. But if the desire is strong enough, and you work hard at refusing to let your disease control your outlook on life, you can still enjoy it to the fullest.

So what does one do? Here a few tips that I've gleaned over the years:

✦ Above all, don't be afraid to communicate. When you start noticing problems with your health that affects your sexual play, speak up. Your partner will most likely understand and try to help in some way, either by making suggestions to make it easier or by introducing a new way that satisfies the both of you.

✦ Go ahead and use belts or Velcro straps instead of rope. I've also used duct tape or plastic wrap for the same effect. Nothing to unfasten; just wrap away, and then either leave a little flap of tape to pull at later or unpeel the wrap. It's just as immobilizing.

✦ Go visit a hardware store or a large home improvement mega-store. There are a wide variety of items that will help. Small padlocks with little keys are no fun to be fumbling with. Use a snap-link, D-link or whatever works for you, but any kind of clasp that fastens whether it has a spring or screws together will work. I love to use leather cuffs for ankles and wrists. I like the spring snap links because it's easy to use my body to produce a little slack in an arm or leg then quickly pop the link in or out of the D-ring in the cuff to release her.

✦ Handcuffs are a kind of fun, but again fumbling around to get the key and unlock them is a hassle. So use the large flex cuffs like cops do. Just leave plenty of slack to use scissors to cut them off later.

✦ If you still prefer rope, take the time to do some research about various slip knots, etc. Keep a tool handy that you can use to open up tight knots if you need to. I still use rope once in a while, and a slip knot usually holds tight enough. If she wriggles too much, it's just an excuse to smack her and admonish her for moving around too much, and I just tie it again tighter. Make little problems like that part of your play; it's always the slave's fault, right?

✦ Again, a hardware store is great for finding alternatives to tight clover clamps or other spring devices. Various sizes of C-clamps can be used instead or large ratchet clamps that can easily be popped open. C-clamps can take the addition of weights as long you tighten them enough.

✦ Crops and whips are a staple of SM play, but sometimes they're not made for those of us that have grip problems. Go find some foam tape used for insulating around doors and windows. Wrap the handle of that switch or crop where the handle is too thin to get a good grip to beat your partner with. I have a favorite rattan switch that I've had for years, but the foam handle is too small to grip hard enough to control it, so I used additional foam tape to make a bigger handle that's easier for me to hold on to.

✦ Shop carefully. It's easy to buy online, but there are implements out there that will work better. Go to a fetish fair if you can to handle the toys to see what's best for you. My two favorite toys now are a multi-bladed cat-o'-nine-tails that was made for me. It has a nice thick handle plus a loop for my wrist that helps. My other is a short twenty-four-inch quirt that I found on eBay for ten bucks. Again, a nice thick handle and a loop makes it much easier to use than the six-foot single tail I started with.

✦ Make yourself comfortable. As my legs grew weaker, we started using the bed more. It was a nice high old fashioned iron bedstead that worked great for us. If I needed to, I pulled up a chair to get between her legs to torment her cunt. If I tied her up to the wall, I'd just sit down with my bag of toys and relax as I weighted her pussy lips or nipples down. Use the kitchen table or countertop — just do a little preplanning, and you'll find the extra time that you have to play will be worth it.

✦ Lastly, don't be afraid to ask others for ideas on how to cope, either online or at your local munch or play group. You'll be surprised to find a number of people that have health issues that no one knows about, and they have to cope with them for sex.

Change is a part of life. No matter how healthy we are now, inevitably, all of us will have to make adjustments as we grow older and our health changes. People are living much longer, and as a result, we're experiencing sex at a much older age than previous generations.

Should we give up certain aspects of our sex life because of that? I don't think so. We still travel and enjoy life as much as before so why should we give up on that? Yes, it may be harder than before and take more time and energy plus the need to take certain precautions against serious injury. For many of us, however, it's who we are; to deny that is to close off a portion of our selves that was important to us. If we shut down a portion of our personality, that may feel like a form of death on its own, and then where do you stop? If you allow that attitude to start, other activities that you enjoy will only fall by the wayside as well. So, as hard as it may be at times, keeping a positive outlook about life, including your secret cravings and desires, will only add to a rich and fulfilling lifestyle.

MK
September, 2011

Finding The Capability Within Your Relationship
Daddy T

A bit of an introduction first: I am known as Daddy_T or KnightHawk in the scene. I have been a switch in the past; however, after my last relationship where I was a collared submissive, I realized that I am better suited for being a dominant. This is partly because this relationship, like every other relationship that I had chosen to enter into as the submissive, turned out to be very unhealthy. But when I am the dominant within a relationship, the relationship tends to last longer and be healthier. I have been in this lifestyle called BDSM/Leather for 20-some-odd years. At the age of 44, I have now earned the title of Master and have been honored with this title by my collared slave and pet.

If I think about where my inability to choose a healthy relationship as a submissive comes from, I find that it goes back to when I was young. I was actually introduced into this lifestyle at the age of six by my father's third wife. There were no sexual relations, but I called her Mistress and was her slave in a very unhealthy manner. This is also where a lot of my emotional disabilities came from, according to my doctors. I have been on SSI since 2007. I struggle with rheumatoid arthritis (RA), fibromyalgia, bilateral carpal tunnel syndrome, bipolar disorder, dissociative identity disorder (DID), slight OCD, and due to a car accident I have two vertebrae that sit side-by-side in my back.

It has been a struggle to find someone who seems to fit with me and with my limitations. I have never really seen them as limitations except in really low moments; I usually see them more as stumbling blocks that I have to find a way around. This has been the difficult part — finding someone who matches my frame of mind and understands how I think. I have grown into a world view of thinking positive and working around my "limitations." I have learned things about myself and about what is and isn't healthy. I find that I am a healthier individual and make healthier choices when I go into relationships as the dominant than when I go into them as the submissive.

When I first met my partner/slave (who is currently known as lil bobbins in the lifestyle scene), she was with someone else, and I was brought in as a play partner and mentor to them both. I quickly learned that her mindset was more similar to mine than to that of her partner of the time. We tried to remain friends, and even played and moved in together for about a year, but I withdrew my offer as play partner to her boyfriend/other dominant because it was becoming too unhealthy for me. I spoke with her often, as we lived together, and still maintained our relationship, but at that time I was battling my illnesses and the knowledge that I couldn't stay in my current situation for a long period of time. I needed to be in a healthy situation with as little drama as possible, and in a clean environment.

When I finally decided to move and find a place of my own, I was gifted by lil bobbin's choice to stay with me. She asked her other dominant to remove her collar and move out. She took my collar, became my full-time slave, and gifted me with the title Master. Since then, we have been working slowly due to her disabilities and mine. I am a very positive-minded person, so I teach her to be one as well. We talk often and work on finding compromises with our disabilities, and on finding useful solutions. For example, if she needs to sleep on the couch because she has to prop herself up due to her back pain issues, then I sleep on my recliner nearby so I am in earshot distance and don't have a closed door between us. This way I am where I can hear her if she needs me or vice versa.

As for the sexual part of the relationship, well, life sometimes takes over with stress and long hours, and we both become too tired for sex even though the desire is there. When we are able to follow through with the desire, there are times that I have to take breaks because of my fibromyalgia and carpal tunnel. Sometimes I have her finish herself off while I cuddle her. I am hoping to one day soon buy or make a fucking machine with different settings. Then when I am unable to continue, I will be able to grab that toy and she can go until she finally reaches that satisfaction point (which for her is hard to reach). It's also easier because we are polyamorous, and a few times we have had another partner with us. In those situations, when I have flare-ups and am unable to continue, I just look to the partner and say "I can't keep up with her tonight. Can you take over?" There are other times I get cramps because of the RA, and we will have to stop and come back to it later, or we just break out into laughter. That is a great thing about this particular relationship: we can laugh! Without laughter and humor we would both be so totally stressed out that we would be crying all the time.

My advice, for what it is worth, for any dominant or slave/submissive who is dealing with a disability is try not to see it as a disability. Try to see it as a roadblock and decide that you just have to find the way around it. Find the activities within and around that road block that add the individuality to your relationship. After all, "disability" is a rather negative word, and as I stated, I like to live in a positive nature and mind frame as much as possible. Lil bobbins and I feel that people with "disabilities" are merely differently-abled. This leads them to be able to focus their spirits and minds in a different way than most people and find the *ability* part rather than the *dis* part.

Never Give Up
Chass

I'm Chass. I'm a 41-year-old white male dominant, and I happened to break my back eight years ago in a fall at work. It cost me my legs, but not my dominance.

I've been into the BDSM lifestyle for twenty years now, and I've been in a 24/7 relationship with my sub for twelve and a half years. I'm a dominant because that's who I am; I like to be in control of all the things around me. I view being a dominant much like being a submissive; you're opening a part of yourself to someone that you might otherwise try to keep hidden. Trust is the key to both sides, for me. (And my D/s relationship also gives me a creative outlet for my sadistic mind.)

When a dominant becomes disabled at a later point in their life — as opposed to being disabled from birth or childhood — I think it's natural to go through a self-doubting and questioning phase. I did that for a while in the beginning, and then I stepped right back in, because it's who I am. The first thing I did to begin crawling out of that phase was to start working on whip control from my chair. Then I slowly learned what modifications were needed to use all my toys. (I do now use quick-releases in all my toys, for the off chance that I fall from my chair.)

As I said, I'm in a long-term 24/7 relationship. We are married and have a small playroom in our house. She has been with me for twelve and a half years, before I broke my back and afterward. She doesn't notice the chair; I am the same dominant man that she once met, and nothing has changed in her eyes. (That's a direct quote from her.) She handled the shift quite well. The fact that I can't walk has not changed me; I am still her dominant and her husband. Frankly, anyone who looks at me and sees my disability first, without reacting to me as a person, will get their walking papers from me.

Service is a big part of our exchange. She takes care of all my needs, as it is her job. My subbie loves to take care of me; it makes her feel valued and needed. Even with that, our relationship is an equal mix of service and control. On days where I'm not feeling well, and I'm in pain or frustrated, it does tend to make me short-tempered. I'm more likely to punish her on those days for taking too long to do something, but she understands and expects this. When it's a real bad day and my pain levels are off the chart, I don't actively dominate her at all. On days like that, she just pampers me completely, and I just take it.

We still play regularly, and I keep finding new ways to manage that. Suspension play, for example, has become a major challenge. I have been modifying things to make it easier, including using some handicapped equipment. I have a hydraulic lift designed to lift paraplegics, and I modified it so that it could also be used as a remote-controlled hydraulic suspension cross. I've learned to modify all my toys in this way. I take the mentality of the dwarves from fantasy novels; they say, "Look to the other side of your tools," which means that all tools can be weapons. Well, in my case, all tools can be toys. I do recommend looking critically at your toys and figuring out how to modify them; you'd be surprised at what you can do. Seek out people who have done it and ask their advice. Never give up!

As far as community goes, it's hard. Locally, there are no BDSM spaces in my area that I can access other than my own. All the munches and such are in people's houses, and none of them have ramps. I recommend that organizers read the ADA rules and regs for public accommodation if they are serious about making things accessible for people. They could also ask those who are disabled about what they need in order to be able to participate.

I'd also like to see fetish photo shoots with dominants in chairs or using forearm crutches. I'd like to see an erotic highlight on those of us who are disabled, dispelling the myth that if we become disabled we are no longer able to be dominant. I'd like to see interviews about how people coped with this or that.

To the submissives who might be reading this: don't look at our disabilities first. Look at our dominance; evaluate that. Ignore the disability and deal with the person. This is why a "courting" period is so important, in my opinion; people have to be together long enough to be able to make an educated guess as to whether they could serve this person through anything that happens. (Also, be prepared for some crazy ideas, because we have to be more creative than the average dominant in order to get our needs met.)

To dominants who have become disabled, I say again to you: Don't give up. You can do it. Adapt, improvise, and overcome. The only thing limiting you is yourself. Seek advice from others who have done it, and get right back in the saddle.

Getting Real
Mistress Tiara

I've always been a dominant person, but disability was a real challenge to my willpower. In my early thirties I was diagnosed with an aggressive case of rheumatoid arthritis. This is an autoimmune disorder which attacks joints, causes inflammation, and also brings a raft of other physically difficult issues of which most people are unaware. I knew nothing more about the condition than the average person before being diagnosed, so it was a sharp learning curve for me.

Just before the onset of my condition, I'd handily acquired a male slave. I choose to believe this was a sign of most excellent judgment on my part, but it's fair to say luck played a really big part in the timing, too. When we met, I was a very active single mother with two children, enjoying life and whizzing around all over the place. My slave was very fit and went to the gym several times a week, but he found even the amount of walking I did in an average day really taxing, let alone childcare and everything else. Anyway, when we met I wasn't disabled. I knew something was going wrong with my body, and I kept going to the doctor, but they dismissed all my odd symptoms as post-partum matters. This didn't make much sense, but that's some doctors for you.

The fact that I was not disabled when we met is very relevant to our overall experiences, and the story I'm about to impart, which is why I'm mentioning it. When Raven asked me to write something for this book, this wasn't what I intended to write about, but upon reflection, the impact of the transition between states has been probably the most difficult matter for us both as a unit and individually. In fact, it's not a stretch to say I have grieved deeply for the things I used to do but can't anymore, for the things I wanted to do but now won't, for the things my slave and I did early on that we enjoyed so very much, for the future we had hoped for and planned, and simply for myself. When I became unwell I felt negated. I used to find myself thinking, "Everyone has forgotten about me," by which I meant the old me, the me I still am inside that had been hidden from everyone's eyes. That was very hard for me. I missed the relationships I had with my loved ones, I missed my life, and I missed the comfort and security of myself as I knew me.

My slave missed me too. He used to whisper that to me in the night when he thought I was sleeping, and I'd often find him staring at me longingly when he didn't think I could see. One of the things he had been drawn to, after all, was my energy. I was the sort of person who always had lots of projects on the go and would look for the joy everywhere I went. *Sunny day? Let's have a picnic! Transport down? Never mind, we can walk. You know that thing you really wanted but couldn't find? Well, I made one for you. That problem that seems overwhelming? Fear not: I've lined up a nifty solution.* I know he still misses my drive and vitality, my energy and my optimism, even now. He misses my take-no-prisoners attitude toward life during the times that it's muted, and I can't blame him because I do too.

We spent much of our early days together on long walks through various woodlands or along beaches. He was far more wealthy than I was at that time, as I was still off work with my beloved baby, and he was used to the finer and more lavish things in life. I introduced him to dusty balmy holidays in countryside caravans, the crisp joy of British beaches, or going for impromptu picnics instead of fancy dinners in extravagant eateries. And, amazingly, he found he actually really loved this way of living, and he thrived. I'd watch him playing football with my two-year-old in a quiet cove in Devon, with its cold grey sea and rockpools instead of the palm trees and luxury pools he was used to, and he looked so happy. He expressed surprise about this many times, but there was no denying that he was finding a contented joy in becoming increasingly immersed in our new life together. (Let us not forget the acrobatic down-and-dirty depravity. Hedonism doesn't even begin to cover it; we were enjoying some smoking hot sex and highly creative kink. God, we had fun.) The reason I mention these things is to explain that he was drawn to my energy; physical, mental and spiritual. It was one of the things he loved about me most, so having these parts of me ripped away or compromised was as hard for him as it was for me.

They diagnosed my RA late, which meant that I was exceptionally unwell by the time I finally got to see a doctor able to treat me, and by the time they started experimenting with different drug cocktails, my slave and I were at the end of our tether trying to hold life together. Then we had to wade through the lengthy process of trying to find medication in the right balance that would help a female in her thirties, with all that that entails. Every day felt as though we were getting repeatedly punched in the face by life, trying to get up and being battered back down again. It was ceaselessly gruelling and exhausting.

Eventually there came a time when I started to doubt whether it was morally justifiable for me to keep my slave. I mean, he signed up with someone different, didn't he? An able-bodied, proactive, young, energetic woman — not this disabled woman with an elderly person's disease and capabilities. It wasn't even like we had been together for decades before everything changed so drastically, with many years of devoted history to draw on. We had only been together a relatively short time when this all occurred, and expecting him to stay with someone he hadn't intended to be with (in this form, at least), in a dismal-seeming situation, seemed profoundly unfair, and as his owner I thought he would be better out of it. I guessed that he would try to honour his word and stay with me, and would do his best because he had said that he would, but I didn't want to do that to him. I wanted him to have a good life without feeling shackled by an obligation to someone who would be a perpetually increasing burden, just because once upon a time he had had a fleeting happy time with them. I felt intensely, painfully saddened by this thought, combined with the additional pain of a massive RA flare, and the stress of mourning my old life. However, I was preparing to throw myself on my sword, because I thought it was the only morally valid choice for all concerned. So I started trying to systematically un-enslave him, believing that this was for his own good.

At about this time I was given a huge dose of steroids to try to quell the escalating symptoms associated with an especially nasty flare, and thus my emotions increased radically and rapidly. (Steroids can do weird things to people.) Eventually I started crying profusely, which is very unlike me. I wanted desperately to keep him, but was determined to do the "right thing" by him, so I resolved to continue with my plan. From my sexy snot-faced sobbing (among other things), at some point he deduced my "ingenious" plan for un-enslaving him. It's fair to say he was most significantly unamused by this discovery. His speech went something along the lines of this:

> "Erm, excuse me, but what the hell do you think you are doing? Since when am I not reliable? How bloody offensive of you to assume I would want to bugger off because you are ill! What have I ever done to make you think I'm that bloody spineless? And as for you deciding I would be better off without you, when precisely did you ask me? Do you think I haven't noticed being a sodding slave is hard? Or that you are demanding and difficult? You are being as judgmental as every prick on the Internet who assumes I'm some piss-poor excuse for a man because I'm owned, and that's not bloody OK coming from you. I'm certainly not going anywhere while you are in this state, and you can forget your cunning plan to un-enslave me, because it's not going to work. It's my job to look after you, and you can bloody well put up with that because you gave me the job. So live with the consequences of your own actions. Consider yourself well and truly bollocked."

While this reaction may not be in the supposed Owner/property handbook, I also couldn't fault a solitary syllable, so for once I wisely elected to shut the hell up. Honestly, quite how one would argue with that without being a total idiot, I am still not sure. I thus decided that if shutting up and accepting both that I was being very stupid and that I am wonderfully lucky meant that I got to keep a devoted slave willing to stick with me however rough it got (and it has got rough sometimes), then I could happily swallow my pride. He took care of me while the steroids were working their way out of my system, and though he continued to be very obviously miffed regarding my earlier cunning plan, he graciously moved on from it.

The event proved to be a definitive watershed moment for us. It was when we got real, when we really truly committed to doing our damnedest to make this work whatever comes, when we realised just how much we meant to each other, and just what we were prepared to go through to keep each other.

We still struggle badly when I am unwell. It makes our lives so hard. I refuse to do the slick, popular thing and say "Oh, it never affects us at all, for we are such a well-oiled machine together that he hardly notice," even though people judge us for it sometimes. We are human beings, with all the fallibilities of the psyche and body that can entail. We are learning clumsily to adapt to the trials we face as a result of both of our health problems. As time is going on, we are improving a little at a time. He has drastically lowered the standards he aims to attain in some areas, and I have finally started to try to let go of what I was and focus on who I can be today and tomorrow. I have also started to let go of my need to always be strong and accept that owning another person means that I can lean on him as I need to. I think he likes that, and he sees it as his job.

If you had asked me before I developed RA, I would probably have said I was mostly a cerebral or spiritual being. Physicality was important, but not as important to who I am as other things, or so I thought. I was wrong about that, and losing much of my physical ability has sent ripples throughout every aspect of our lives and thus our relationship. My careers have been more intellectual than physical, and perhaps this is one reason that I was so easily fooled into underestimating my physicality. But oh, how I like doing things with my body! I like to cycle, I love dancing, and I love to run around as though I am far younger than is seemly. I like very aggressive sporting activities. I am a very sexual creature, and I'm very sadistic. On reflection, I have now realised that these things come from a specific energy, while simultaneously creating that energy for me. It is cyclical and really goes to the heart of "me".

Being weak (which is what I feel like, even if others don't perceive it that way) doesn't suit me, and try as I might, I think I will never fully adapt to it. I don't *want* to bloody well adapt to it. I'm at least being forced to adapt my coping mechanisms, though. That is the best I can do, and it helps maintain a balance for me between doing what is necessary and not compromising the essence of myself. It has meant that I am no longer willing to focus on attaining my future goals so thoroughly that I will compromise our todays. Now is what counts, more than ever. We are here today, and today matters to me more than the maybes of tomorrow.

Is my disability an Owner/property issue? Not on the surface, but it's had far more impact on us as an Owner/property pairing than anything that would be clearly called an Owner/property issue. That I own a loyal, competent, hard-working slave has undoubtedly been a blessing when it comes to rolling with life's punches. He sees it as his job to carry us where I can't; he sees that as his duty as my slave. This is a matter that people sometimes do not understand — that he responds this way as part of his slavery, not as something in opposition to it. When he comes home exhausted from the job he now has because I can't work properly (a big change after some blissful time with him spending time as a stay-at-home slave) or drives me to a hospital appointment, he is being my slave even more so then when he is kneeling prettily. He is slaving, and that takes dedication.

The events around my health declining brought our baseline into sharp focus and impacted every bit of our lives. He's owned, and that's the end of that. We have both gained a deep certainty of our bond, and there is a quiet peace in that knowledge. I believe that his hard work in adapting to my needs has made him a better slave. He has had to let go of some facets of his ego (which I suspect might have otherwise remained intact much longer) to facilitate really focusing on the job in hand, because that's what the job takes now. I own him and I know he is going to keep trying, and that's something special as far as I am concerned. I may be disabled now, but despite my personal qualms, apparently I am still worth a hell of a lot of effort.

The Master's Vision
Jeff Harrison

I am a 49-year-old master with a slave, and I have been
blind since I was a very small child. I was born prematurely
and got too much oxygen in my incubator, and it ruined my
eyes. It was a common cause of blindness in the 1950s and
early 1960s. I could see a few colors and vague shapes until
about the age of 5, and then I was completely blind and no
longer even remember what those vague visual experiences
were like. I grew up with this condition, and while I am
fairly skilled at taking care of myself and getting at least
some things done, there will always be some areas of life
where I will need a lot of help to be able to do anything at all.

For years, I depended on the kindness of friends to fold
my money, read me my phone bill, read me books that
weren't on tape, and help me get around in non-urban areas.
I had a few girlfriends, and I always explained that
unfortunately, doing these things for me kind of came with
the job of being in relationship with me. Some of my lovers
were fine with helping me out — at least when they were in
a good mood about me — but it was always difficult, even
when they loved me and cared about me. I tried to return the
favor in as many ways as possible — making them breakfast,
bringing them tea and toast when they were ill, things like
that — but it always felt like the relationship made more
work for them than it did for me. And, in almost all cases,
when they broke up with me, they echoed that sentiment.

I often attracted confident and somewhat controlling
women who wanted to mother me and saw me as a "soft"
man who would complement their own harder natures.
Some were more maternal about it, but a few were outright
pushy and would set about trying to make my life better. The
problem was that I would go along with it for a little while,
mostly in the first flush of falling in love, and then I'd dig my
heels in and rebel. We'd fight, and I'd have to reestablish my
boundaries. I tend to be quiet and reserved, and I can be very
tender with someone when I'm in love, but I'm not
submissive. They mistook the combination of my demeanor
and my disability — and, to be fair, my desperation — to be
submission, and were then surprised when they discovered

that I'm actually an Aries, and I don't like to be told what to do. Fireworks would fly, they would back down, and then the cycle would repeat itself. One female friend in whom I confided pointed out that my disability was subjecting me to the kind of assumptions that women get just from being female — people would assume that just because I was blind and not very outgoing that I would submit and do what I was told, and they would move in and try to make me do what they wanted, just as men assume that of any woman who isn't incredibly assertive.

One particularly fierce, brilliant and dominant (though not maternal) woman had a fiery affair with me for two years, during which we broke up and got back together a couple of times. She'd promise not to be so pushy and then find herself inching in that direction anyway. Towards the end of it, she learned about the BDSM community and started going to munches, and then she decided that if she had a slave, she would have somewhere to put her dominant urges and wouldn't be shoving them onto me. She found herself a slave in short order, but the result was that we spent more time apart and finally broke up amicably for the final time. I talked to her slave about BDSM and master/slave relationships, and I was intrigued. She and I finally had a late-night conversation in which she suggested that I might be happier if I had someone whom I could dominate, although she wasn't sure how I would find a partner. For that matter, neither was I.

I went with the two of them to a play party or two, but again I felt like people assumed that I was a submissive because I was being led around by these two friends (one of whom was clearly a dominant woman). The state of being blind was conflated with the state of helplessness — and thus submission — in their eyes. As for myself, I could hear all those cries and sex noises, and once I got over the idea that inflicting pain was wrong to do to someone even if they craved it, I wished more than ever that I could see what was going on. Play parties are a very voyeuristic situation, but since it is considered extremely rude to touch anyone without their permission — and, for that matter, to ask to touch someone when they are in scene — I was set apart, yet again, from all the people having fun. In addition, I did not apparently put across a dominant enough "aura" to attract any submissive women to my lonely perch at the edge of the room.

At the same time, I was admitting to my own fetishes. First, there is my thing for long hair. Nothing gets me hard like the feel of long hair — the longer, the better — sliding through my hands or brushing across my body. I love to feel it brushing against me while I have sex, and I love to grab fistfuls of it, hard, when I come. (I've talked to a number of blind men and discovered that this is actually a fairly common fetish of ours.) I fantasized about being able to fuck a prone woman, laying on top of her, while I yanked her head back by her long hair. Most of my lovers had been long-haired women, and while they let me play with it, I wasn't allowed to be rough. I told myself that it was wrong to want that ... but I still masturbated to the idea.

After the failed attempts at finding partners at play parties, I resorted to Internet ads, and that's where I found my first two submissive play partners, and eventually my slave. The first two women I played with weren't interested in being lifetime subs — they were players, and actually switches who were less threatened by my quiet demeanor. They taught me how to top a woman — how to tie someone up, how to use clamps, and how and where to smack them. You're thinking right now that no one could possibly whip someone else without seeing them, but you'd be wrong. I can't stand several feet away and flog someone, but I can certainly hit them up close with a short strap or smaller flogger, as long as I first find the area I'm striking with my hand. Spanking, of course, is no problem at all, especially if someone is across my lap. I'm very aware of where things are in the space around me, so once I find someone's ass with my hand, I know exactly how to come back to it in a split second.

I also learned how useful sensory deprivation can be when you're topping someone blind. To blindfold them, or to put them in a completely darkened room, means that I know where things are better than they do. They'll stumble around, and I can hunt them by the sound of their breath and their footsteps. It's a mindfuck for them to be completely without vision, to be pounced on in the darkness, to be wrestled down, restrained, and hurt — and, yes, fucked. I prefer to have all my scenes in my spare bedroom, which has covered windows and no light fixture. In a lighted area, they can see me fumble around for toys and condoms. In the pitch dark, I am the master and they never know what's coming.

While my two play partners taught me a lot about BDSM, I still wanted more than that. I wanted a life partner who would be willing to be submissive to a blind man. Just when I'd given up on the idea altogether, I met Kim over the Internet. We had a courtship period of cyber-dominance, and I was almost terrified to let it end, because I was still afraid that she wouldn't be interested once she actually met me. After all, I didn't even know what *I* looked like, much less what I would look like to her. I didn't want to seem like one of those fake doms who never want to meet in person, though, and if she was going to reject me for something I'd already talked to her about repeatedly on the phone, I wanted to get it over with. I still remember sitting there in that cafeteria, my heart in my mouth, wondering which footsteps might be hers. Actually, she moved so quietly that I couldn't hear her until I heard a soft voice saying, "Sir?"

Our first conversation went wonderfully, and I asked her if she was willing to go shopping with me. Shopping, especially in a crowded, noisy mall, is an ordeal for me, and I figured that it would be something of a service trial-by-fire for her as well. She told me that she would be happy to do so, and I showed her the best position for leading me around. She commented on how wonderful it would be to have a master who didn't make her walk behind, but whose hand she could always hold. At that point I knew that I wanted to keep her. Halfway through the shopping trip, after she had deftly guided me around the crowds, read me everything I asked her, folded my change into the proper denominations, and referred to herself as my "seeing-eye brunette", I knew that this was going to work. We went home that night, and I put her in the dark room for about half an hour, tied up. Then I came in and played with her, and took her.

She was my slave from the next morning on, and we've been together for more than two years now. Kim lives with me and is my assistant for all the things I need. I don't have to feel like I'm inconveniencing her, because serving me is part of who she is. She's come up with ideas to please me that I'd never thought of before, like describing colors in terms of smells and tastes and temperatures, or dividing the food on my plate with carrot sticks or celery garnish, or finding me an onion-chopper that is safer than a knife. She spends several hours a week reading to me, which we both love and look forward to; I've been able to broaden her literature horizons, and she's been a gateway to my hearing books that I can't find on tape and wouldn't otherwise be able to know.

I advise her, and I'm patient with her — I'm good at being patient; I have a lifetime of practice. A few months into our relationship, I told her that she was beautiful — we had just finished having a scene and I was holding her sobbing in my arms and stroking her hair — and she burst into harder tears. When I asked her what was wrong, she told me that part of the reason she had been attracted to me was that she felt herself to be fat and unattractive, and she had figured that I wouldn't know. She felt like she was fooling me, and that she should inform me that my slave was actually an ugly woman. I took her waist-length hair in my fist and bent her head back, and told her that I was the only one whose opinion mattered now, and that she was to think of herself as beautiful from now on, because I believed that she was. Her self-image didn't change overnight, but we've worked on it and it's much better now.

I was quite pleased when I found out that Kim likes camping and the outdoors. I love to be outside, and hear and smell the wilderness, but camping is fraught with difficulties for me. I don't know where anything is and the ground is covered in danger. It's hard for me to move a foot from the tent. Kim is happy to walk me anywhere and describe everything to me; she loves to see me touch everything, smell everything, listen to the birds, and be happy in my discovery. So she has been my doorway to nature as well. I swim well and I've gotten her over her fear of water — I had to, because I wanted to go out on boats. Now we can canoe across the local pond — I provide the muscle for rowing and she steers. So we have enriched each others' lives.

I never did get a service animal — I thought about it, but they are very expensive, and I could never afford it. Now I have a seeing-eye brunette who is my eyes for everything. She shops for me, because she can read ingredients. She pays the bills because she can read them, but I tell her how much to pay each month. She cleans the house and puts everything right back where it goes, except for her room which she is allowed to keep messy because I never bother to go in. With her as my slave, I can do just about anything. The world is open to me. I've often mused to Kim that every blind person should have a slave, but she just laughs and tells me that not every blind person is dominant. Maybe so, but I am a very lucky man, and would be whether I was disabled or not. I'm the one with the vision of what we should be, and she follows my lead in life, just as I follow her lead on the street. It's a perfect synchronicity.

Serving A Disabled Dominant

On Serving A Disabled Dominant
Rave

My Sir is a Shaman, Husband, Boy, lover, partner, boyfriend, top, and Master to various people. Oh, and he's disabled too.

Before I took up with him, I never considered myself a "service submissive". Sure, I had previous D/s relationships where I carried things for them and got them drinks, but I wouldn't have considered myself "in service". When I first began this relationship with my Sir, my thought process was more like, "Hey, if I help carry stuff and help him with his classes, I'll get to go to this event!" He was also into edgier and darker kinks than I'd had experience with, and into energy-work in kink, which I wanted to explore. However, as our relationship grew, I came to realize how happy I was when I had honestly worked hard for him and done a good job, and all I wanted was to be a good "girl", for good service or some semblance thereof. It was a big change of perspective for me.

When we first started talking about a D/s relationship, he was very honest about his condition. To the outside world he appears "normal", but the everyday average person doesn't see some of the challenges he faces. He has a chronic illness that gives him pain, fatigue, and difficulty moving around. Serving him has been a challenge for me, because in my head I want to do everything I can for him to make his life easier, even occasionally the things that he is perfectly capable of doing himself. I sometimes fear that he thinks I see him as an invalid, which I don't, but I want to do the little things for him so that he will have the "spoons" to do the important things. His condition changes from day to day, and on some days he can do more than on others. I have to walk a fine line in order to serve him without overstepping the boundaries of what he wants help with on any given day.

My Sir is a teacher and presenter to the Pagan and kink communities, which means he travels whenever his health allows it. Presenting away from home at events can be challenging and energetically draining for him. My service to him — whether it is carrying things, doing administrative work, or being a demo bottom — allows him to do his work and focus his energy, time and physical presence on being an educator. My job is to see that he doesn't have to worry about the little things — like where his next class might be or where he can find something to drink — and to be in the background giving whatever service and tools will make his life easier.

I have actually benefited in many ways from serving him. I am generally an impatient person, but dealing with my Sir's challenges has taught me to slow down, be more patient, and remember that my actions reflect on others. When I walk with him, I might need to walk differently — more slowly or more vigilantly. I have a really bad short-term memory, so I've learned to plan and make lists, which makes it easier for me to remember stuff. When we are at an event, I prefer to have a full schedule and specific jobs to do. I dislike randomly wandering about, and because I'm shy and kind of socially awkward, just hanging out with friends or acquaintances for hours on end used to be weird and boring because I would run out of things to say. I say "used to", because being with Sir has taught me that silence can be a good thing, and some of the most informative conversations I've been in have come from just sitting around and hanging out.

If I were to suggest a list of tips for the service submissive of a disabled master or mistress, I might list:

+ **Anticipatory Service.** Through observation, learn to anticipate their needs before they need them. If you watch them and ask questions, you can learn their preferences, whether it be food, drink, or the type of chair they feel most comfortable in. If you plan ahead, those little things can make their life a lot easier, especially when they know that they don't have to worry about it. Find out what their favorite comfort items are, whether those are food, a kinky toy, a stuffed animal, or anything else; if they are having a "bad day", having that favorite item might make it easier.

✦ **Traveling and Events.** If you are going to an event or hotel-based trip and your Master has mobility issues, check to see how accessible the hotel is. If they have dietary restrictions, check local restaurants to see if there is food that they (and you) can eat, and plan for how to get to those restaurants from the hotel.

✦ **Have a plan, but be OK with throwing it out the window.** There might be times during traveling when they are having physical challenges and may need to leave earlier than expected. Just be flexible with your plans and realize that it's not all about you.

✦ **Be able to entertain yourself.** Sometimes my Sir will say something like, "I'm having a rough time, and I just need to not focus on anything," and he will turn on his computer or watch TV, and he just needs quiet. So I'll have my laptop, journal, or small handcrafts to occupy myself without being a bother, but I'll still be around in case he needs something. (You could also work on service projects during this time too, such as cleaning or organizing.)

✦ **Medication.** If they are on medications, find out what dosage and frequency they are taken, and what the side effects are. In addition to medication reminders, if you know what they are and when they are to be taken, or if an urgent medication is suddenly needed you can recognize and fetch it. By researching their effects, you can understand which ones are not as urgent as others, or which ones are new, and what side effects need to be watched for. I suggest having emergency contact info on one or both of you at all times during your service. My Sir carries a flash drive in his wallet with all of his medical information — doctors' names, phone numbers, all the medication he takes, and his medical history.

✦ **Equipment.** My Sir occasionally uses a wheelchair for long walking distances. When I first started pushing him in it, it took me a while to be able to estimate the dimensions, so maneuvering around doorways and corners was difficult until I became more experienced (and I might have run over some toes in the process). Learning how to use any equipment they might have,

perhaps early on during some down time, will save
time later.

✦ **Learn their triggers, in order to avoid additional
issues.** Do they like a particular style of chair to use? If
so, it might be helpful to bring that style of chair with
you if at all possible. If they have low-energy issues,
maybe you can suggest building in some extra down
time during events in order to recharge. Recognize the
signs of possible health problems and have an "easy out"
that they approve of ready to hand — for example, if
they are stuck talking to someone oblivious, and you
can tell that they need to rest, you could discreetly step
in and remind them of a meeting/class/date/whatever
to allow them to move on .

✦ **Learn how to pack and carry effectively.** If I learn to
pack better, I can fit more in the car and still have room
to see out the back. The reason I mention this is that if
you pack well, you can not only carry more things, but
you also won't have to make a lot of trips back and
forth, and you can accompany your master into your
destination and open doors instead of being stuck
behind with the luggage. I've found that I can carry
several smaller bags and still be effective, but dragging
one large suitcase doesn't really work well.

✦ **Be willing to go to an event in their place, if
necessary.** Sir, his husband, and I frequently travel to
events together, whether they be family, kink, religious,
or others. However, sometimes he decides he is unable
to go due to health reasons. When this happens,
sometimes we all stay home, but sometimes he might
send me or his husband (or both) in his place. If this is
something your master requires, you need to be able to
represent them if they aren't able to make it, and act in
a way that would reflect well on them.

Being in service to a disabled Master has really been
the best thing that has happened to me. It has been an
incredible journey. He might have good, bad, and great
days/weeks/years in the future, but my job is to support
him on whatever journey he has to make, in whatever form
that service might take. I have benefited so much from Sir

— he has given me education, training, friendship, forgiveness, and great play. Through him I have learned patience and a new perspective on life and the world around me. I am honored to call him Sir, and it makes me happy to hear a "Good girl!" for a job well done. I still have a long way to go, but I'm happy to take this journey with him.

Serving Him

Pyora

I'm Pyora, and I am a 44-year-old female submissive who is married to her dominant. We've been married for eleven years, but have only been in a D/s relationship for the past seven years. We are 24/7, which is not quite what most people seem to think it is. It's not being in a scene 24/7 — to be honest, that would burn us both out and it's really not feasible. We're more service-oriented, and we have a child together. To avoid giving our son a skewed idea of what a relationship should be, we tend to use code words and phrases to alert each other to what is a command or not a command. My own disabilities tend to limit positions that I can be in — for example, with the condition my knees are in, kneeling is a short-time-only situation, and we have actually developed a pad for me to kneel on when I do kneel.

My Master is a paraplegic; he has no use of his legs and is in a power chair. His disability has no impact on how I view him, either as a dominant or as a husband. His image of himself is that he is dominant, regardless of his legs; it's his mind that matters, not his body. He does have high pain days, as well as occasional bouts of depression, but he tries to not let it get to him. He feels that he must be a good role model for our son, and he can't be a good role model if he just sits back and vegetates.

We met and married before the accident that left him paralyzed from the navel down. I was extremely "vanilla" when we got together, and he attempted to leave that part of himself behind to avoid scaring me. Still, I picked up on bits and pieces and started researching the lifestyle; he eventually caught me doing the research and we discussed what each of us felt it was all about. By the time we actually began a D/s relationship together in addition to the marital relationship, he was already in the chair, although he'd been very active and involved before we met. The D/s relationship was nothing new to him, but it was actually more of an adjustment for him than for me, because I was learning how to care for him at about the same time I was learning about being his submissive.

Most of our activities have required an element of modification that wasn't there before, both for sex and for scening. We've both learned that modifications are key, and that they're not really as hard as you'd think. One example is that he insists on an easy release for all restraints, in case he has a spasm that throws him out of the chair; I am always able to release myself and assist him back into the chair without having to be an escape artist. Being his medical caretaker, I am in a service position much more than most submissives are likely to be, and he does not have to work to come up with services for me to perform. I have had to learn a number of medical procedures that I would not normally have had to deal with. One position that I find myself in is having to push him to do something to take care of himself, but it's still serving him by getting him to take care of himself so that he is able to be served.

However, it is also important to us that I can take care of him without falling into a mindset where I'm the one in charge and he's the helpless invalid, even when I am doing services for him that might be seen by outsiders as infantilizing or disempowering. It helps that it is just so much of his personality that he is dominant (and so much of mine that I'm submissive) that we just don't cross that line. Another part of it is that we both keep in mind that it's done on his orders. Even when I have to make him do or take something he'd rather not because it's medically necessary, I am still performing service for him by taking care of him. I remind him that he must take care of himself so that he can play with his "toys". If he is in too much pain or too ill from refusing to take care of himself, he can't enjoy individual time with me — and, worst case scenario, he could end up in the hospital.

Physically bad days are a common thing for us; the biggest change is that it increases the service side of the D/s relationship and decreases the sexual side. Service tends to play a large part in our power exchange relationship. A large part of my service to him *is* caring for his physical and medical needs. I'd say that our relationship is more service-oriented than his power exchange relationships in the past, but it's as much about control as it is about service.

Most of the play parties in our area are in private homes, which are not wheelchair accessible unless they have someone in a wheelchair in their own family, which is not the norm. We really don't take part in our local BDSM community due to this, and also due to the fact that the closest public meeting place is a hundred- mile round-trip drive. For event organizers, I'd start with recommending that the physical facility is at minimum wheelchair accessible, with access to a handicapped accessible bathroom, preferably one that allows a caretaker to assist without putting both in an uncomfortable position. If this is a public event with advance notice, mention something in your advertisements. Encourage disabled individuals (whether the dominant or the submissive) to contact the person making arrangements in advance with their specific needs and modifications that might be needed for participation. Most individuals with disabilities either bring along or provide their own modifications to meet their physical needs (as long as the facility is accessible) or are able to give you specifics about what is needed to enable them to participate.

Even in the D/s community we still tend to hear "How can he be a dominant if he's in a wheelchair?" Being dominant is not related to your physical status, it's more of a mental state of mind. Regardless of whether the relationship is more service-based or more control-based, it's still up to the dominant to be imaginative and creative, and I've noticed that disabled dominants tend to be even more imaginative and creative than those that aren't. The best way for people to realize that dominance is more mental than physical is to actually interact with those who are "differently abled".

For subs who are wondering about serving a disabled dominant, I do have to say that you're likely to see less physical submission and more service and mental control. Take your time, get to know the dominant and make sure that you are compatible, and that serving them is what you really want to do. Realize that, at times, serving them may potentially put you in a position where you must tell them they have to do something in order to serve them to the best of your ability. For example, my dominant requires injections. He cannot give them to himself due to the placement of the shot, so I must give him the shots. The problem is that he does not like getting his shots and will attempt to put them off if he can, so I have to push him to go ahead and let me give him the shot. I also do have to be flexible; if he's having a high spasm day, I might have to wait until his spasms ease or even potentially wait until the following day to give him the shot. I do *not* want to chance breaking a needle off in his body.

I wish people could simply realize that a disabled person is first and foremost a person. Their disability is not who they are or how they identify themselves. Also, realize that not all disabilities are visible. There are plenty of disabled dominants out there who look physically "normal" but still need a lot of good service in their relationships.

The Caregiver Slave
Joshua Tenpenny

Eleven years ago, I was a service-oriented submissive looking for a master to serve, and Fate brought me to my master Raven. I figured that I'd be a houseboy, or a general all-purpose assistant, and indeed we started out that way. Raven is an author (of 32 books to date), an educator, and a presenter in several different communities — not just the BDSM or kink communities — and he needed a PA to follow him around and make sure that he had his notes, call cabs, pack and unpack, and generally handle all the details. He also needed an extra pair of hands around his farm, and the fact that I could build websites was a plus as well.

We dated long-distance for a year, and I was impressed with his energy and willpower, and all the projects that he was involved in. I moved in after that first year, which was a decade ago, and I live in his little farmhouse with his wife and other housemates. Raven has medication-resistant lupus (systemic lupus erythematosis), which gives him chronic joint pain, various food allergies, a compromised immune system, and a host of other symptoms. He has a hiatal hernia, skeletal malformations from a genetic endocrine disorder, a mild case of Tourette Syndrome, and occasional tonic-clonic seizures. When we met, the lupus was largely in remission, he had very good control of the Tourettes, and the seizures almost never happened without warning. He told me he'd been very sick in the past, but neither of us got into this relationship thinking of him as disabled in any way.

In about a year and a half, his lupus (which is incurable and often progressive) got much worse. He was sick frequently, and often exhausted. He almost always needed a cane to get around, and sometimes a wheelchair. Some days he couldn't walk or bathe without assistance. He would wake up in the middle of the night ill or in pain and would need my help. The arthritis got bad enough in his knees and ankles that it eventually caused his knee to give way while braking in the car. This meant that he had to stop driving, and I became his chauffeur. He'd enjoyed having me drive him places previously, but now it was a requirement.

I'd started out as his personal assistant, but within a very short time I became his personal care attendant. Fortunately, our relationship was based primarily on my willingness to serve him, not his ability to control me, so I didn't see this as a significant change in my role. There was a little discomfort for both of us, though, because I was suddenly thrust into a situation of more responsibility than either of us had expected. I went from chores that wouldn't matter much if I failed at them to responsibilities that literally held his well-being in my hands. Neither of us were really ready for the level of trust and commitment that these new roles would require, but there wasn't time to develop that trust slowly. It needed to be done, and we did it. There wasn't much choice.

He still kept teaching at conferences when he could (and still does), but my presence was no longer just a helpful option. I remember an incident about two years into our relationship when Raven was travelling on business in another state and I was left home to take care of the goats. He called me late in the evening in the middle of his trip, telling me to get the spare keys for his truck and meet him as soon as possible at a certain bus station two hours from our house, where he had arranged an emergency ride from a friend driving through. He told me to bring a warm blanket, a thermos of hot tea made with specific herbs, and a few different medications. He didn't give me many details of what was going on, and I didn't ask. I just assembled everything and drove to the bus station.

When he arrived and was dropped off, it was clear that he was in terrible shape. He'd begun a severe lupus flare on the first leg of his trip, and it had become bad enough that he'd been forced to leave halfway through. He wrapped himself in the blanket, drank the tea and took the meds, lay down on the seat, and told me to drive him home and put him to bed. I did, again without asking. As he lay in bed later, he told me how wonderful it was to have that kind of unquestioning obedience when he was that ill. Other egalitarian partners, past and present, certainly would have helped Raven in a situation like that, but they would have done it on their own terms. They would have wanted to know more of what was going on, given him their opinion on the situation and whether this was the best way to handle it, and wanted him to take their advice on the matter. I just did what I was told, as exactly as possible, and that kind of help was just what he needed in order to manage his condition. He was going to use me to take care of himself, and I would become his auxiliary hands. Having control over his life is important to him, and this was a way he could have some control over the situation. It's hard enough for him to cope with so little control as it is.

That night was a turning point, in that afterwards he trusted me with all his PCA duties — because he knew that I would do exactly what he wanted without argument. That was also the last business trip that he took alone. Since then, I've traveled with him to carry luggage, set things up, find him special food, check ingredients in restaurants, push his wheelchair on the few occasions that's been necessary, and render whatever health care aid is necessary to keep him functioning and on his feet while he is working.

Raven had a very hard time coming to terms with his illness. He'd always been very self-sufficient (and more than a little stubborn) so as he became progressively more disabled, he'd still try to do his normal activities. If he was just a writer in a city apartment, I think it would have been easier, but he was accustomed to splitting firewood, milking goats, building sheds, and keeping a huge garden. As each activity was pushed beyond his ability, he had first a period of denial and then a period of mourning. Being dependent on someone else, even if that someone was his slave, was very hard for him.

He tried all the conventional medical treatments, but had very little success, and eventually the doctors gave up on him. They sent him home and told him to check into the hospital if his organs started failing, and perhaps they would try chemotherapy at that point. His comment on the way home was, "To hell with them. I'm firing the lot of

them. I can do better than this." He threw himself into
alternative health care treatments, including changing his
diet, getting acupuncture, taking herbs and supplements,
getting more sleep, avoiding the sun, and doing a lot of
energy work. He was actually worse than he'd ever been at
that point — his acupuncturist confessed years later that he
had "a very scary tongue" when he first came in — and his
liver had taken some damage from the lupus. He had
several bouts of pneumonia and pleurisy that were entirely
from his own immune system attacking his lungs.
However, by a year later, he had pulled himself back from
the edge and his lupus was now only chronic and annoying
and painful, but no longer dangerous. I went from thinking
"My master is going to die!" to "No, my master is just
disabled, and we can handle this."

Part of his plan to use me as a tool to heal himself was
to send me to school for massage therapy, complementary
health care, Thai yoga massage, and acupressure Shiatsu.
That story is told already in his essay, so I won't repeat it
here blow by blow, but it bears repeating that part of
creating the perfect slave for a disabled master can be
getting real training in health care or health aid skills. It's
one of the sharp differences between the "butler porn" style
of service and real, down-to-earth, dire-necessity service.
We kid about how I wasn't trained to be a slave at some
mysterious European House O' Slavery, but at the local
community colleges.

It's not easy when Raven is at his worst, physically.
When someone is experiencing continual pain, fatigue,
and physical limitation, dealing with that uses up a lot of
their mental and emotional resources. It didn't upset me at
all when Raven couldn't get out of bed or walk, but when
he was too exhausted or fuzzy-headed to make decisions, I
didn't know how to cope with that. I would see him refuse
to make decisions on small things, and I would think, "He
can't even decide on this little thing! What will happen if
something big comes up!" Over time, however, I learned
that he wasn't just being passive or avoidant; he had his
own thought process going on. His disability fluctuates
wildly, but even when he is in bad shape he is still capable
of dragging himself up by an act of sheer willpower and

facing down a huge and important decision. However, he really isn't willing to waste that much effort on small decisions that could be put off; his priorities are such that recuperating and getting back out of the flare are more important than small decisions that might loom large in my eyes. We've always found that things just go smoother when I accept his priorities and his decision as to what is a big deal and what's not, so that's what had to happen with this situation.

In the context of healthcare and human services, I've often heard a distinction made between "caregiving" and "caretaking". These aren't explorations of the dictionary definitions of either term, but a call to examine the different ways people act when taking care of others, and to promote a healthy and mutually respectful relationship between the people involved. There is no consistent definition used for either term (aside from "caregiving" being the better one), but there are certain recurring themes that are relevant to any service-oriented person in relationship with someone who has a disability. Ideally, a "caregiver" is encouraged to see themselves as someone who is offering services and support, which the patient has the right to refuse, rather than taking control of their health care as a "caretaker" might.

Much of the distinction centers on the patient's right to self-determination. Up until recently, the conventional model was that the health care professional had all the answers and told the patient what to do. The patient was the passive recipient of services, and was graded as "compliant" or "noncompliant" with treatment. The "good patient" did what they were told without asking difficult questions. However, as author and surgeon Dr. Bernie Siegel points out, "good patients" also obediently die on schedule when given a terminal diagnosis. It is the "bad patients" who refuse to be treated like an object and insist on being in charge of their own treatment. In Dr. Siegel's experience, it's also the "bad patients" who have miraculous recoveries. In addition, health care professionals are coming to understand that lifestyle changes are essential to managing many chronic diseases, and passive patients rarely implement those changes. Disability activists have also done a great deal to convince professionals that taking a parental role with physically disabled individuals is demeaning to them. This is slowly changing the focus to a caregiver model, where the professional offering services is aware that they are not there to manage the patient's health.

This distinction is crucially important when dealing with a disabled dominant and their submissive servant. Because of the social baggage of the conventional model of health care, both parties in an M/s relationship may still tend to see the role of the servant as a caretaker, which undermines the foundation of the relationship. If I could impress one thing on submissives who serve disabled dominants, it would be this: you are not their mother or father. Don't act like you are. Ever.

It is not easy for a dominant personality to accept help that they don't want to be needing in the first place. It's hard for them to ask for help when they want to do it themselves, and if they actually do ask for help, the worst possible outcome is when the "help" isn't really all that "helpful". It's hard enough for them to trust that you'll be able to give aid competently and respectfully; if you don't do it the way they want it done, that will make them less likely to call on you in future. They may also feel that your taking care of them will change the dynamic.

I find it beneficial to avoid seeing these services as something that the dominant is incapable of doing for themselves — even if they technically are — and instead see them as activities that the dominant wants the submissive to do for them. (As one woman who uses a wheelchair commented, "I don't *need* a wheelchair. I could crawl around on the floor, or have four buff, shirtless men carry me down the road. I *choose* to use a wheelchair because it is a more convenient way to get around.") If both people are able to mentally classify these activities in the same category as any of the other services that the dominant might want, from making coffee to doing a striptease, it will reinforce rather than undermine the dynamic.

With the right attitude on the part of the servant, personal body care can be framed as a luxury service and not a symbol of infirmity. All the way up to the 1800s, it was customary for the upper class to have servants who dressed them and bathed them. A medieval king probably never put on his own clothes except under battlefield conditions, and possibly not even then. A Roman magistrate had slaves to scrub their body and comb their hair. If you can tie doing bodily care to the idea of a servant to a lord or lady, that may help both parties to better accept their role.

One of the pitfalls that I see in submissive-type people is that they are more interested in taking care of others than of themselves. They can have a tendency toward martyrdom, but this is counterproductive. If you need support to keep yourself healthy, get it. Try to get enough sleep, food, and exercise. Obviously, your master is going to decide on your schedule (if you live together and that has been negotiated), but don't pretend that you don't need these things when you actually do. Be honest and ask for appropriate time and space to care for yourself; a good master will be happy to help manage that. It is a useful quality to be sturdy enough to do without these things for a short period of time when it's absolutely necessary, but it isn't a skill that needs to be practiced on a daily basis. Your suffering isn't serving anyone here. It isn't a measure of how good a job you are doing. Instead, you should be proud of the quality of your work and how much it benefits your dominant. If nothing else, your dominant may notice that you do a better job when you are taking care of yourself.

Another trap that the submissive should not fall into is needing to be needed. Some people are attracted to relationships with disabled or damaged people and would prefer that their partners not be self-sufficient, because being needed badly makes them feel more secure. They might worry that if their partner didn't need them, they would be thrown out, or that they have no value besides what they can do for people. People with this issue tend to feel threatened if their partner's condition improves.

However, a dominant partner is more likely to appreciate a submissive who can help them to be more self-sufficient and find ways that they can do tasks themselves.

As a final point, I'd like to put in a word for keeping things sexual, if only in little ways. Even the most well-meaning caretaking relationship can become desexualized if both parties sink into an "invalids and cripples don't have sex" mindset. There are so many small touches that you can add to what would otherwise be an uncomfortable or perfunctory act — a sensual caress in passing, a quick kiss on the feet or other part of the anatomy, kneeling whenever possible to do lower-level activities, leaning your head on their shoulder or knee as you adjust something, or being a support with body language that says "footrest" more than "helper". When someone is in chronic pain, sex may seem more like an effort than a fun time, but we've learned to remind each other that it can help pain — or at least take his mind off of it — for a while. For difficult days, we've worked out ways to have sex that don't require him to do anything but lay in bed. I can put on a show for him while he orders me around, or I can get myself into a position where I can do all the work, but he can still decide on the activities. A small thing like being gagged or plugged can completely change the tone when the submissive is being the active partner during sex. And never underestimate the value of a good blowjob (or whatever) for helping to relieve what would otherwise be a very bad day.

It is very fulfilling to me to know that what I do for my master benefits his life so much. Having done this job professionally, I am also delighted to know that at least one disabled person doesn't have to settle for a PCA who only steals from them occasionally or is only a jerk to them when they're drunk. Seriously, I love it when I can figure out a way to lessen some of the pain and misery in his life. I know that I can't fix him — and it's not my job to try — but I know that he's been dealt a more difficult hand than many people, and when I can alleviate any part of that, I feel like I'm the best boy ever.

Serving The Chariot Goddess
Kainey

It was the afternoon of the Gay Pride Parade. We'd finished walking the route, and I was standing in line at a refreshment kiosk to get drinks for myself and my mistress. I heard them talking, at what I assume that they assumed was out of my earshot, but I have exceptionally good hearing, and I could get pieces of the conversation. They were appalled about my costume — a ponygirl in full harness with a bit in my mouth — and that I'd pulled my mistress in the parade. On the other hand, they argued, there was the fact that my mistress was in a wheelchair, and she couldn't actually walk. (And four miles is a long way to self-propel even if you are a crip with a decent upper body, I'll tell you right now.) So, they reasoned, there might be a point to her being pulled, but did it have to be by an obvious slave? Couldn't she just be a quiet, decent cripple, being sedately pushed along by some volunteer? (They didn't exactly say that, but I could read the subtext.) Did she have to make it into some kind of imperialist oppression? (They did use *those* words.) Did we think that oppression was all right if it was between two women? Part of their discomfort was seeing me in a subservient role, but I could tell that some of it was also discomfort with the idea of a crip — and a crip woman — in charge. And not just in charge, but completely dominating someone else. Surely, they said, this was done because of some huge insecurity on her part. Some insecurity caused by being a crip.

I wish that I could have walked out of line and told them how wrong they were. I wish I could have faced them down and told them that's just the way she is, that she would be dominant whether her legs worked or not, that she would still want to be in charge. I wish I could have told them that it isn't about her being insecure, but about her being confident, and that I wasn't so stupid that I couldn't tell the difference. I'm not attracted to insecurity. I'm attracted to survivors in the larger sense, to people who have been up against terrible odds and are still tough as nails and no one tells them what to do. That gets me hot, and melts me into a puddle of submission ... but I was being a good girl and standing in line to get tacos and lemonade, so I just stood there and stewed.

Zoe is the love of my heart, and the mistress of my body. She is a L4 spinal cord injury survivor, from a car accident in her teens. She is brilliant and tough and kinky and loves women. We have been together for eight years, and I couldn't imagine life without serving her. I met her over the Internet, and we had cyber-domination for months before I moved to her area. She was completely open with me about being in a wheelchair. By the time I met her, she had had many years of coping with her disability. She lives in a disability-accessible apartment with a roommate, a gay crip man who is a sub. (He hasn't found anyone yet; he is under her protection, and she screens bad influences for him.) They both work for the same electronics company. Moving in with her was a big adjustment, because so many things are set lower. It's almost more convenient to kneel all the time.

In a lot of ways, our relationship is an ordinary master/slave thing. I do call her my mistress. I know that some dyke dominants use the word "master", but she says she isn't quite butch enough to be comfortable with that. Neither of us are really butch or femme; we just tend to go around in jeans. She used to wear skirts because they were easier to put on, and that was before she got on Depo-Provera shots so she doesn't have to have periods any more. Now she has me to help her get into jeans, and she can wear tall boots with lacings because I sit on the floor and lace them up. She likes those when we go out because they help keep her ankles from flopping over. I clean the parts of the house that are hard to reach and do chores that are a pain for Zoe and Gary to manage. I cook because they are both bad at cooking. I hang laundry, and I work to help pay rent.

We refer to her chair as her chariot. Chariots were the ride of kings and queens, gods and goddesses, and charioteers who were superstar athletes in ancient days. We've sprayed it in colors and put ribbons in the wheels. Sometimes I push Zoe's chariot, when she's tired, but she's in good shape — she has great arm muscles! — and usually she wants to move herself. Sometimes I walk beside her and carry things. Sometimes she wants to carry things and I push; it depends on her mood. I've learned not to suggest one mode or another. It's important to her dignity that she decides how her chariot is handled at any given time.

The chariot is often the scene of our sex. There are sometimes chains attached to various places — the handlebars, the arms, the footrests. They are discreet, but they are for attaching me to the chair. The first time we got together, she tied my ankles together so that I couldn't walk, and then attached a chain from a collar to her chair. Then she wheeled around her house very slowly, and I had to crawl along and follow. Afterwards, I understood a little more about her.

Someone once posted a picture to the Internet that had sixteen positions for wheelchair sex. I think we tried all of them. Some worked and some didn't. My favorite is being on her lap when she has a cock strapped on, facing away so she can grab my nipples and call me names right in my ear. I also like being across the arms of the chariot with her beating my ass. She doesn't have much sensation down there — a little, but not enough to have orgasms — so I guess you could say that she's stone. However, she loves to make me come, and she says that if I'm up against her, she can feel my orgasm through my body. Sometimes she makes me go down on her because she likes how it looks. I do it after I clean her off, sometimes.

Her lower body is my responsibility. She gave that to me as a gift when she collared me. I take it seriously. She will never have a pressure sore so long as I am her slave. Every night I inspect her and make sure that nothing is chafed or raw. If it is, I clean and bandage it and put on Vitamin E, and make sure that part of her chariot, or her clothing, is padded until it is healed. I rub the seams of her jeans until they are soft, I tape cotton to the inside edges of her boots, and I tape padding to parts of her chair. Her bladder and bowel control is so-so; it depends on how tired she is. Usually she can make it to the toilet, but on days when she can't it's my job to take care of it. She says nasty-sexy things to me while I clean her up, so I don't feel like a mom changing a kid's diaper. She makes me kneel and kiss it all after she's clean. In the beginning, if she thought I was acting like a mom, she would make me kneel and kiss her while she was still dirty. That put me off being maternal really fast. I am her slave, not her mom or caretaker.

Some people have said that part of their master's job is to protect them, and that they couldn't be with someone who couldn't fight off gangs of rabid rapemongers. Maybe those women were all victims of terrible physical assaults, and were still so wrapped up in that experience that the main qualification they need a dominant to have is the ability to prevent a future iteration of that trauma. Maybe. But I am not a victim of rape and physical assault. I'm a victim of a lifetime of people who said cruel things to me, or tried to pressure me verbally, or who otherwise used their words and their will to make me do or feel something I didn't want to do or feel. I have some social anxiety, and I will stand there flustered and speechless while people take advantage of me or verbally abuse me.

Zoe doesn't put up with that for a minute. No one ever makes her speechless or flustered. She looks people in the eye and puts a stop to their games. She doesn't need to be able to throw a punch to protect me — she does it just fine with her eyes and voice alone. Once a ramp broke while she was trying to get from one floor to another in a store, and the manager came over to sweet-talk her and make sure that she wasn't going to sue them. She looked him in the eye and said, "If you're going to talk to me, you're going to do it on an equal level with me. Now sit down." She used the same voice on him that she uses on me, and he sat. That made me so hot that if we hadn't been in a store, I would have dropped and kissed her feet.

So it depends on what kind of protection you need. She will call people up for me when I'm scared to talk to them. If we're in a crowd and I get flustered, she notices and takes over talking. When we're out together, everyone looks at her and not me anyway, so I can blend in. She's my protection just by being there.

When play parties or munches or meetings are held at people's houses, there are problems getting there more often than not. I call ahead and ask if the site is accessible, and often I have to explain what that entails, because people don't know. They think that a couple of steps up ought to be OK, as long as it isn't a flight of stairs. Sometimes we can get her over a couple of steps, sometimes we can't, depending on height and room. It's impossible to figure that out over the phone, so sometimes I've dropped by earlier in the week to check it out. Flights of stairs and no elevator is a deal-breaker, unfortunately. People have offered to carry her up, or have a bunch of people carry her up chariot and all, but I don't think they understand how undignified the first option is and how dangerous the second one might be. She always turns them down.

When we find a party we can play at, we bring our own folding table to put her gear on. People tend to have a lot of standing furniture, like crosses, and not a lot of low furniture. Tables need to be lowered so she can work on me. If there's nothing we can use, we just find a hook and tie my hands overhead while I kneel in front of her. The footrests on her chariot make a good spreader bar when they are shoved between my thighs.

One of our protocols is that when we are home alone and I am within ten feet of her, my head is not allowed to be higher than hers. That was actually my idea. She thought it was kind of silly, and inconvenient for me, but I pointed out that she had to crane her neck for everyone else all day when she went out, so wouldn't it be nice if she never had to do that for me when we were home? We tried it, and she liked it so much that it became a rule. So when I sit with her at home, I sit at her feet or in a shortened chair or a little bench. When I come up to her, I bow or drop to my knees. Sometimes if she is blocking a door, I get down and crawl past her. It makes her smile and it gives me a chance to drop a kiss on her feet. She likes to watch me kiss her feet although she can't feel it.

I'm not a really large or strong person, so I can't lift her in and out of her chair. She can generally lift herself onto some surfaces, but sometimes it's difficult — like getting onto and off of toilets sometimes when she's tired. We worked out a way for me to help her that doesn't require me to be strong, just sturdy. I kneel in front of her and get myself centered with my knees spread wide, and then put her legs over my shoulders. She leans forward and puts her weight onto my shoulders so she's sitting on me for the moment, and I hold her ass and she grabs onto my hair, and then I swivel my torso and deposit her where she needs to go. Most personal care attendants wouldn't do that move, because it's kind of submissive and puts my face right in her stuff, not to mention the hair pulling. Which makes it just right for me.

Another move, to get her onto the ground (like if she wants to lay in the sun) without having her fall out of her chariot, is for me to get on all fours facing away, with my ass under the chariot. She slides forward onto my back and then I collapse carefully, getting her to the ground. We refer to these two techniques as Pony 3 and Pony 4. Pony 1 is me pulling her chariot, and Pony 2 is me pushing her chariot. I came up with these positions from watching a show on disabled horseback riders who had trained their horses to get down on the ground so they could mount, then carefully stand up. "I can do that," I said. So now I have gloves and knee pads in the kit on the back of her chariot. And I shaved my head on both sides, like a long mohawk, but people don't know that's because I am her pony.

I'm proud to be her slave, her girl, her pony. I do feel like helping her is doing something good for the world, but it doesn't come from a place of her being a poor little thing who needs help. If she saw me acting like that, she would slap my face and say things that put me in tears. I like that she can do that. Before you think that she's an awful bitch, I should say that she is almost always very, very good to me. She holds me in her arms at night, calls me her girl, and tells me I am beautiful. She kisses me when I am crying and snot-nosed from being beaten and tells me I am beautiful. However, I know that if I'm a bitch to her, she will be a bigger bitch and put me right down. If I treat her like she is a poor little thing whom I am so generously helping, she will grab my belt and drag me down till she can reach my hair, and then she will throw me on the floor by my hair, and then she will put me in my place verbally. I think that took maybe four times and I never did it again, but I know that she could do it if she wanted to, and that is sexy to me.

Strength has nothing to do with bodies. It's about what's above the neck. My crip mistress is so strong that she puts me to shame. I can be envious, or I can be a part of it by being a part of her. That's what I chose, and I don't regret it. Ever.

About the Editor

Raven Kaldera is a queer FTM transgendered intersexual shaman who is often seen with a cane and occasionally with leg braces or in a wheelchair. He is the author of too many books to list here, including *Dark Moon Rising: Pagan BDSM And The Ordeal Path* and *Power Circuits: Polyamory In A Power Dynamic*. He and his beautiful and useful slaveboy Joshua have been teaching and presenting workshops regularly for many years to the BDSM, Neo-Pagan, Sex/Spirituality, transgender, and a few other communities. He sees his physical challenges as just another obstacle to overcome in his quest to change the world whenever possible. His slaveboy Joshua refers to himself as "a wholly owned subsidiary of the vast enterprise that is Raven Kaldera." 'Tis an ill wind that blows no minds.

www.ingramcontent.com/pod-product-compliance
Lightning Source LLC
Chambersburg PA
CBHW031522270326
41930CB00006B/492